SIX MAKERS OF ENGLISH RELIGION

1500-1700

The author: Gordon Rupp is professor of ecclesiastical history at the University of Manchester, England. He lectured in America in 1956 and in 1952 was an exchange professor at Emory University in Georgia. Rupp is the author of important studies of Luther and PRINCIPALITIES AND POWERS. He is associate editor of the Library of Constructive Theology series.

SIX MAKERS OF
ENGLISH RELIGION
1500-1700

by

Ernest GORDON RUPP

HARPER & BROTHERS, PUBLISHERS
New York

Copyright © 1957 by Ernest Gordon Rupp

Printed in Great Britain

Bible

TO

MY BELOVED UNCLE AND AUNT

AND MY AMERICAN COUSINS

CONTENTS

INTRODUCTION

MUCH of this book was given as a course of lectures to "non-theological" students at Westfield College, in the University of London. It seems invidiously negative to define a group of students, and such an alert and pleasing audience, by what they do not study, and it had better be recorded that most of them were in fact arduously pursuing an Arts degree. But I suppose that "non-theological" is less a description of an audience than a warning to the lecturer not to get too involved in technical matters, to avoid the jargon of the schools, and as far as possible not to oscillate between the obscure and the banal. I fear I have fallen short in all these matters, but such as they are I offer these pages, less as technical studies than as edifying discourses. I hope they may encourage some readers to study for themselves the great "best sellers" which are the object rather than the subject of this book. I say object, because I have put first, not the books, but the men who made them. It seems important to remember that great traditions are not made in the end by books and words, but by men and women.

I will not hide from any reader that by "English religion" I intend in the first place the "English Protestant tradition". But that is not intended polemically or in a sectarian fashion: for though as somebody said of great Bernard Manning, I am of the cavalry rather than of the foot, and have a rather Irish way of trying to be eirenical, "Protestant tradition" for me is part of the communion of saints, that flow of corporate life within the one People of God. When a century ago the men of the Oxford Movement recovered for the English Church an awareness of the holy tradition, they had the defects of their virtues, and one of those defects was an inability to look at the Reformers fairly and squarely: regarding the Protestant Reformation as a disastrous interruption, even a perversion, of Christian continuity. I think there is room for a more generous perspective, and have in mind among the kind of readers I desire those who rejoice to be both Catholic and Protestant, who will not be ill pleased to remember that George Herbert was nourished on the English Bible and Prayer Book, and that Nicholas Ferrar loved to read from Foxe's *Book of Martyrs*.

A way of life was created in England by the Reformation, and it contained a way of faith which was different from the mediaeval religion which preceded it, and the pieties of Continental (and Scottish) Protestantism, and of the Counter-Reformation, and post-Tridentine Rome. You cannot analyse a tradition: like a coral reef, it has a million tiny cells, in this case the lives of millions of humble, believing men and women. But in the making of English Protestantism there are certain landmarks, certain great normative documents. Such were the English Bible, the Book of Common Prayer, and in a lesser way Foxe's *Book of Martyrs*, *Paradise Lost*, *Pilgrim's Progress*, and the hymns of Isaac Watts. All were writings which influenced many millions of readers. All had behind them the creative energy of genius. Three of them belong more particularly to the Establishment, three to the Nonconformist pedigree, but in fact they have affected the temper of all English communions and afford, even in separation, an example of Christian "growing together".

I do not feel too apologetic about their Protestantism. For though I usually tell my Catholic students that we shall get along very well if they remember that roughly I mean by "Protestant" what they mean by "Catholic", I mean something else as well. And in these days when a virile Roman Church is less aptly symbolized by Bunyan's gibbering, toothless, senile Giant Pope than by some stalwart tough (with padded shoulders!) playing football for Notre-Dame, the Protestant religion still seems to me worth living, fighting, and dying for. And I think there is matter in these pages which may be an antidote to some forms of ecumenical romanticism, and cut across some of the complacent assumptions of a literary world which seems a little crowded with the descendants of lapsed Dissenters.

The chapter on Cranmer was read as a paper to the John Mason Neale Society in the University of Cambridge, and is a tribute by a non-Anglican to him, at the fourth centenary of his death. I have to thank the Principal of Westfield College, Dr. F. Chesney, for much kindness, and the staff and students for courteous encouragement and patient listening.

GORDON RUPP

UNIVERSITY OF MANCHESTER.
January 1957.

CHAPTER I

WILLIAM TYNDALE AND THE ENGLISH BIBLE

THE creative, religious ferment in the English Reformation has been sadly underestimated by modern historians. The great Acts of State which disrupted the ancient bodily connection between the empire and church of England, and the mediaeval Christendom centred in Papal Rome: the subtle, forceful pressures of economic revolution: the competing commodities of warring politicians and aspiring gentry—these have held the centre of the stage, and the reformers themselves, when not depicted with spleeny hostility, have been dismissed as "small-time stuff". Well, we need not underrate the importance of Henry VIII and his divorce, but if the "light that shone in Bullen's eyes" is a factor in modern history, so also is the twilight in a Flemish prison, where a shivering, coughing scholar peers at Hebrew words in the falling dusk. In the long run, the supreme fact in the reformation under Henry VIII was a religious fact, the making and opening of its Bible to the English nation.

Since Archbishop Arundel's constitution of 1408 it had been forbidden to make or read any translation of the Bible not authorized by ecclesiastical authority. The surviving copies of Wycliffe's Bible, and of Purvey's more polished version, had mostly been confiscated, and shorn of their heretical encumbrances had attained respectability among the guarded treasures of religious houses. There were little groups of Lollards who survived into the 16th century, the "known" or "just fast" men living in villages along the Chiltern hills, the Thames valley and in Essex. Theirs seems to have been a simple, pious, anti-clerical religion, and the evidence from the bishops' courts suggests that they had only a few tattered, precious copies of single gospels and epistles which went the rounds from one congregation to another. The vivid story in Foxe, of how some of these Lollards from Steeple Bumpstead visited Friar Robert Barnes during his "house arrest" in the London Austin Friars, and there argued with him about the merits of the new translation, reminds us that these groups were an eager constituency for a new version of the vernacular Bible.

Then there were the scholars. There were groups of younger men in Cambridge, and, after a colony had been transplanted by Wolsey to his new college in Oxford, in Oxford also, and these were marked by their bent towards Biblical study. They believed that the Bible ought to speak for itself, and that its text and meaning was not to be submerged in the intricate systems of the late schoolmen. When John Colet in Oxford, and George Stafford a little later in Cambridge, began to lecture from the plain scriptural text, they roused hostility by their novel methodology as much as by anything they said. They were not alone: across Europe, in the universities and at princely courts, and the great publishing houses, groups of forward-looking scholars turned with a new zest to the revived study of "the sacred languages", of Greek, Hebrew, and a renovated Latin. They made the basis of their exegesis of Scripture the text itself, philologically interpreted on the basis of the best manuscripts. And the leader of this new generation of humanists, with its zeal for "sacred letters", the great Erasmus, came first to Oxford and then to Cambridge.

It is tantalizing that we know little of his direct influence on those he taught in England. Only one or two in later days boasted of having been his pupils, and perhaps he was not the last distinguished foreign scholar rather to misfire in our often surprisingly insulated academic societies. But if his personal influence is doubtful, his New Testament was a sign and a portent. It was in its way a manifesto, the embodiment of the new humanism in its restive opposition to an addled scholasticism. And Erasmus did not hesitate, in 1516, to speak very boldly indeed of his hopes for the spread of Bible reading, in his famous hope that the gospels might be read by wayfaring men, "that the husbandmen may sing parts of them at his plow, that the weaver may warble them at his shuttle". The younger dons at Cambridge, always susceptible to mental fashions, went after the new Latin text which Erasmus produced in 1519. "I bought it," confessed Thomas Bilney, "being allured rather by the cleaner Latin than by the Word of God." Cleaner or no, it converted him soundly, turned him into a Reformer and set his feet towards his martyrdom in 1531.

Erasmian humanism was that of scholars and intellectuals, a class not given to breeding martyrs. Huizinga has finely described the Erasmian ideal as that of the good conversation of a group of friends sitting in a garden. And it is a noble emblem of the flower of culture: it appears and reappears in history: Sir Thomas More and his friends: Dr. Johnson and his circle: S. T. Coleridge and his allies: Augustine and his companions in the garden at Milan, and Socrates and Plato and their disciples. Indeed it might be argued that the Bible both begins and ends the human story with conversation of friends in a garden.

But the Bible also reminds us that corruption and death break in upon our human cheerfulness, and that often the luxury must be interrupted, postponed, sacrificed for a generation. Certainly some twenty-five of these young Cambridge men were to come to the fire in the next decades. They did not press for a vernacular Bible, for they delighted in the new linguistic tools, and the book lists of proscribed books which they bought show that they were mainly after the new Latin Biblical commentaries of the 1520s as they stemmed from that remarkable German, Rhineland, Swiss ferment, the commentaries of Luther, Melanchthon, Oecolampadius, Bucer, Zwingli, Hedio, and Lambert of Avignon.

There are mysterious references to a "Society of Christian Brethren" which has been described as a kind of "Forbidden Book of the Month Club". It seems to have been an organized sodality with its own accounts and auditors. It subsidized scholars like William Tyndale, and it underwrote the dangerous but not unprofitable godly trade of smuggling into this country the works of the Reformers from 1520 onwards, and then from about 1526 a whole spate of English religious literature. Merchants like William Petit, Humphrey Monmouth (Tyndale's friend and patron), Richard Hilles, were men of standing, of the Livery of their Companies, sturdily anti-clerical and not above attending secret meetings to hear the Scriptures read, like the curiously modern sounding "night schoole" in Friday Street delated to Sir Thomas More. The books were printed in Cologne, or Strasbourg, or Basel, sold at the great book fairs at Frankfurt, sent up the Rhine on barges (itself a hazardous business, for there were many inquisitors on the watch), then shipped over to England in bales of cloth from Antwerp or Hamburg, to London or Bristol or the port of Lynn in Norfolk. Then began an adventurous journey under the guidance of some colporteur, who risked his life taking the books to where there was most demand for them, to the universities of course, but also to certain great religious houses like those of Bury and at Reading. They provoked fierce counter-action from the authorities. Many of the book agents were caught, some tortured and some burned, like Richard Bayfield: others like George Constantine recanted in a whole flood of recriminating evidence about their former friends which was good cannon fodder for the polemical artillery of Sir Thomas More. There is now evidence that Luther's works were being sold in England in 1520, but it is half way through this fateful decade that the work of a group of English exiles gave the English Reformation a direction of its own, and among them the chief was William Tyndale.

William Tyndale (1494-1536), whom More called "the

captain of our English heretics", was born in Gloucestershire, and educated at the grammar school attached to
Magdalen Hall, Oxford, and then in the Hall itself. Foxe
says that he went on to Cambridge, but there is no evidence
in any Cambridge records. There are gaps in our knowledge
of his career, and we should like to know who taught him
and what books he read, and whether his teachers knew
that he was more than a student with an unusual flair for
languages. He then became tutor to the young children of
Sir John Walsh at Little Sodbury, and like another humanist
with linguistic gifts, the German scholar Spalatin, he also
may have chafed at having to accommodate his mind to
kindergarten from research, and to teach the rudiments of
grammar to little boys. There Tyndale made his first
translation, significantly a rendering into English of
Erasmus's *Enchiridion*. There also he got into trouble with
the local clergy. We do not know when and how the thought
came to him to make an English Bible. But he came to London and sought in vain the patronage of Cuthbert Tunstall,
Bishop of London.

He sent him a specimen copy of his translating, a rendering of a Greek oration of Isocrates, but if Tunstall saw it he
did not see in it any premonition that here was one whose
fame would outlast his own scholarly renown (for he was a
maker of mathematical textbooks). It is not certain that
Tyndale made known to him his hope that, under episcopal
patronage, he might begin a Biblical translation. If he did,
it was an unwise move. For humanist though the bishop
was, and friend of Fisher, More, and William Latimer,
and of Erasmus himself, times had changed since the
appearance of Erasmus's New Testament. For one thing
it had come under heavy fire from Catholics at Louvain,
and from the English scholar Edward Lee, one day to be
Archbishop of York. And for another the spread of Luther's
heresy, whose writings had infiltrated England since 1520,
had made all the authorities hypersensitive towards
dangerous novelties. At any rate, Tyndale was courteously

B

rebuffed. He did some preaching at St. Dunstan's in the West and there found more solid patronage from the London merchant Humphrey Monmouth. Here, living plainly, he stayed for six months at his studies. It is possible that at this time, through the German merchants of the Steelyard, he got hold of Luther's new German Testament, and it may be that he began to learn to read enough German to use it as a tool.

At any rate, his project became sufficiently formed for it to be expedient for him to leave this country, and he went accordingly to Hamburg, with grateful assistance from Monmouth, and a grant from some London merchants of the kind who later maintained the "society of Christian Brethren". Although Sir Thomas More, Edward Lee, and the German Cochlaeus said so, and Mr. J. F. Mozley has made a gallant attempt to demonstrate the fact, I still think it probable that he did not go to Wittenberg, but stayed in the Rhineland. In 1525, it is true, Bugenhagen's letter to the English saints from Wittenberg was written and translated into English, but I should attribute it to the work of William Roye, who matriculated in Wittenberg later in 1525, and who dabbled much in vernacular translations. Roye was a gifted linguist, who may have been the scribe of the Leicester Codex of the N.T., a Greenwich Observant on the run, and a man with a talent for boasting and indiscretion. Tyndale had perforce to use him, as colleague, in getting the New Testament into print. It may have been Roye, as Mr. Mozley suggests, who, in his cups let fall the secret of the Tyndale Testament to the eager hearing of Cochlaeus, who caused the authorities to seize the sheets as they were lying in the house of Peter Quentel in Cologne. The result was that only a fragment, mainly of St. Matthew's gospel, was printed in 1526 and of this only one copy is known to survive.

Baffled, but not in despair, Tyndale fled with Roye to Worms, and there in an octavo (the Cologne fragment was a folio) edition his New Testament finally appeared. Spalatin (who would surely have met and known Tyndale had he been in Wittenberg) reports the comment of his friend Buschius at this time in a famous entry in his diary:

> Buschius told us that at Worms, six thousand copies of the New Testament have been printed in English. The work has been translated by an Englishman, staying there with two other Britons, who is so skilled in seven tongues, Hebrew, Greek, Latin, Italian, Spanish, English, French, that whichever he speaks you might think it his native tongue.

We ought not to press details of a bit of gossip, but we cannot help remarking that this is a very odd list and does not include German. And though it is probable, as most writers assume, that it refers to Tyndale, it would fit Roye (in his boasting) much better. For Roye was born in Calais and had from his youth not only a foot on the Continent but some knowledge presumably of French. Roye soon left Tyndale and made for Strasbourg, with another runaway Observant, the red-headed Jerome Barlow, where he indulged in "railing rhymes", and translated an exceedingly interesting Strasbourg catechism, dying according to one story, a few years later in Portugal.

Only two copies have survived of Tyndale's first New Testament, which Mr. Mozley calls "the greatest treasure of all English printed Bibles". Of the signal merits of this work of genius there need be no question. Professor Butterworth says that in the lineage of the English Bible

> chief place of honour is undoubtedly Tyndale's. To Tyndale we owe the tone of simple earnestness, the plainness of speech, the economy of words which characterize so much of our Bible.

It has been estimated that of the words used in Tyndale's New Testament 90 per cent. have survived into the Authorized Version and 75 per cent. into the Revised

Version. He was limited by his tools, but he used the best
he could get: the new versions of Erasmus, the Latin of the
Vulgate, the German of Luther. He kept the order of
Luther's Bible, which placed Hebrews, James, Jude and
Revelation at the end, and his preface in this and later
editions drew heavily upon Luther's, so that there was some
colour for the Catholic outcry that this was simply an
Englishing of Luther's Bible. Of course it was not: and Mr.
Mozley gives many examples of Tyndale's originality and
independence. Despite its quaintness and its archaisms, it
reads well and with a rhythmic quality missing from many
modern versions, as he will find who cares to read it aloud
perhaps from the beautiful edition published by the Royal
Society of Literature in 1938.

The version was immediately attacked. It appeared at the
time when the authorities were highly alarmed at the infiltration of heretical literature. There had already been
public burnings of Luther's works. At both universities
there had been arrests and investigations. The ambassadorial visit of the famous "hammer of heretics", John
Faber, for a few days in 1527 had no doubt led to important
conversations between him and his English humanist friends
Fisher, Tunstall and More. But it was Sir Thomas More
who became Tyndale's great opponent, even though More's
controversial writings reveal the least noble side of a great
Christian Englishman. The words of C. S. Lewis about
More's polemic are worth remembering:

> He is monotonously anxious to conquer and to conquer
> equally, at every moment: to show in every chapter that
> every heretical book is wrong about everything—wrong
> in history, in logic, in rhetoric, and in English grammar
> as well as in Theology . . . to rebuke magnificently is one
> of the duties of a great polemical writer. More often
> attempts it, but he always fails.[1]

Tyndale was a reformer: in all great matters save perhaps

[1] *English Literature in the 16th Century*, p. 174, O.U.P., 1954.

in the doctrine of the eucharistic presence he agreed with Martin Luther. He was enlisted in a great debate which was bitterly engaged on both sides of the channel, in which at this very time his dearest friends were grievously and fatally entangled. He too hits out, and hits hard, and perhaps you would no more guess from polemical Tyndale, any more than from polemical More, the goodness and integrity, the generosity and humour, which was common to them both. Tyndale's other writings are tiring and repetitive, but he is, as C. S. Lewis says:

> like a man sending messages of war, and sending the same message again and again, often, because it is a chance if any one runner will get through.

Tyndale himself knew how tentative this first translation must be. In his preface he avowed his own incompetence and begged for assistance in its progressive emendation. Yet he little deserved the howl which went up from conservative quarters, that it was heretical, unscholarly and bungling. The charge of heresy rested on two points; first, that he had rendered traditional words, technical terms which had an established sanction in ecclesiastical tradition, by novel and unfamiliar usages. It is a charge always brought against all translators, but in the 1520s it was dangerous. Tyndale had indeed rendered church by "congregation": priest by "senior" (afterwards, in 1534, by "elder"): "do penance" by "repent", and "grace" by "favour" (though there are a hundred passages where he retains grace as a translation of "charis"). More serious was the charge brought against the later editions, of the glosses and marginal notes, often of a fiercely polemical kind.

It is true, as Mr. Mozley says, that a plain text without glosses would have been unthought of. But there is no doubt that such marginal notes provided the authorities with a wonderful smokescreen, behind which to evade the theological challenge of the "open Bible".

In the first place, some philological notes were necessary. Erasmus had to insert many notes of this kind in his version, and got Oecolampadius and Capito to help him with the Hebrew. In an age without plain commentaries, explanations of a philological kind were necessary. Moreover the state of the English language was such that almost any English version must use words unfamiliar in some parts of the country, and Mr. Mozley finds in Coverdale at least 140 completely new words. And there were points of information, like the famous note in the Bishops' Bible about the gold of Ophir. (Psalm 45. 9):

> Ophir is thought to be the Ilonde in the West coast of late found by Cristopher Colombo: from whence at this day is brought most fine gold.

When we come to anticlerical polemic, it is not always realized how much fiercer are the notes already to be found in Erasmus. Thus Erasmus on Matthew 24. 23, "Lo, here is Christ . . ." says:

> I saw with my own eyes Pope Julius II at Bologna, and afterwards at Rome marching at the head of a triumphal procession as if he were Pompey or Caesar. St. Peter subdued the world with faith, and not with arms or soldiers.

And on 1 Cor. 14. 19, on worship in an unknown tongue:

> They have so much of this in England that the monks attend to nothing else. A set of creatures who ought to be lamenting their sins, fancy they can please God by gurgling in their throats. . . . Boys are kept in the English Benedictine college solely and simply to sing morning hymns to the Virgin. If they want music let them sing Psalms like rational beings, and not too many of them.

There were few things in the glosses of the first English Bibles which had not found rough expression for long enough in all levels of society from the Court to any London tavern.

From the point of strategy, the glosses may have been a mistake, but we must understand that for the Reformers the Bible could not be isolated from the whole matter of reformation. And yet Tyndale saw further than many of his friends. There is a famous letter from Stephen Vaughan, Cromwell's agent in the Low Countries, in which he tells of a meeting with Tyndale and an attempt to entice him to return to England by an offer of pardon:

> I perceived the man to be exceedingly altered, . . . in such wise that water stood in his eyes, and answered: "What gracious words are these. I assure you," said he, "that if it would stand with the King's most gracious pleasure to grant only a bare text of the scripture to be put forth among his people . . . be it of the translation of what person soever shall please his majesty, I shall immediately make faithful promise never to write more, nor abide two days in these parts after the same: but immediately to repair into his realm, and there most humbly submit myself at the feet of his royal majesty, offering my body to suffer what pain or torture yea, what death his grace will, so this be obtained."

Tyndale revised his New Testament in 1534. After the setback of a shipwreck in which he lost precious books and manuscripts he translated, with the help of Miles Coverdale, the first five books of Moses: and there is reason to believe that he made a translation of the next section of the Old Testament, from Joshua to Chronicles. But in 1535 disaster came. He had lived as a pensioner, if not as a chaplain, in the house of the English Merchants in Antwerp. There he was betrayed to the Imperial authorities by a fellow Englishman, Henry Phillips. From his last captivity a letter has survived which breathes the spirit of a Christian scholar:

I beg your Lordship and that by the Lord Jesus, that if I am to remain here through the winter, you will request the commissary to have the kindness to send me from the goods of mine which he has, a warmer cap: for I suffer greatly from cold in the head, and am afflicted by a perpetual catarrh which is much increased in this cell: a warmer coat also, for this which I have is very thin: a piece of cloth too, to patch my leggings. My overcoat is worn out: my shirts are also worn out: he has a woollen shirt if he will be good enough to send it. I have also with him, leggings of thicker cloth to put on above: he has also warmer night caps. And I ask to be allowed to have a lamp in the evening. It is indeed wearisome sitting alone in the dark. But most of all I beg your clemency to be urgent with the commissary that he will kindly permit me to have the Hebrew Bible, Hebrew grammar, and Hebrew dictionary that I may pass the time in that study. In return may you obtain what you most desire, so only that it be for the salvation of your soul. But if any other decision has been taken concerning me, to be carried out before winter, I will be patient abiding the will of God, to the glory of the grace of my Lord Jesus Christ, whose spirit (pray) may ever direct your heart. Amen. W. Tindalus.

So Tyndale worked in the dusk until the night came. His work was unfinished, and like the heroes of the Epistle to the Hebrews he died seeking things to come. He was strangled and his body burned in the town of Vilvorde in Brussels in October 1536, and though so many 16th-century last words are suspect, it is credibly told that his final cry was "Lord, open the King of England's eyes."

Butterworth says that "in the line of scholars who made the King James Bible, the name of Coverdale stands second only to Tyndale". He was born in Yorkshire, and became an Austin Friar in Cambridge, where he studied under the Prior Robert Barnes. In 1528 he left England and helped

Tyndale with his translation of the Pentateuch. His own first translation seems to have been an edition of the Psalms by Campensis, a solitary copy of which survives in the library of Lincoln cathedral. Then, in 1534, he was induced by a Dutch merchant to try his hand at a version of the whole Bible, and this he achieved, by October 4, 1535, issuing two revised versions in 1537. In 1540 he went to Strasbourg and at sometime received a D.D. at the University of Tübingen. He had married a noble Scotswoman whose sister had married the professor of theology in the Danish University of Copenhagen, a family connection which was to be fateful for him.

He was a pastor as well as a linguist, and for a time became teacher and minister in the Alsatian town of Berzgabern, returning to England as Almoner to Katherine Parr, in the reign of Edward VI, and a great doer in the West of England during the tumults of 1549, so that he was rewarded for his energetic preaching by the bishopric of Exeter, August 1551. When Mary came to the throne the authorities were in a difficult position, with England excommunicated and with the Edwardian legislation unrepealed, and any kind of legal loophole was seized upon to silence the leading reformers. In the case of Coverdale he was charged with non-payment of the first fruits of his diocese. But he had friends at another Court, and the repeated intercessions of his kinsman by marriage brought him the support of the King of Denmark. He is the one first-rank Edwardian reformer to escape the fire, and he went first to Wesel and then to Geneva, where he helped to make the Geneva Bible, and like other framers of that book, he did not return immediately to England on the death of Mary. Geneva perhaps indicates the radical temper of his mind, for he would on no account return to a bishopric, nor was any high preferment given him, until in 1546 he became rector of St. Magnus, London Bridge.

His was a careful, modest and thorough mind. He was no linguistic prodigy like Tyndale, but he had great virtues, of which the lovely translation of the Psalms in the Prayer Book are eloquent testimony. His Bible was advertised as "truly translated out of the Dutch [i.e. the German] and the Latin".

His sources were fivefold: Tyndale's New Testament and Pentateuch, Luther's German Bible, the Latin Vulgate, the Latin version made by the Italian Dominican Pagninus in 1528, and the Bible of the Swiss Reformers of Zurich. Mozley says "that in his translation he leans heavily on the German, pays much less heed to the Latin and uses Tyndale freely".

On August 4, 1537, Archbishop Cranmer wrote to Thomas Cromwell about a version of the Bible which had come into his hands and which he thought might be licensed, "until such time that we the bishops shall set forth a better translation, which I think will not be till a day after doomsday".

This new Bible was the work of John Rogers, the friend and literary heir of Tyndale, and a former chaplain at the English house at Antwerp, though it is known rather mysteriously as "Matthew's Bible". John Rogers (c. 1500-55) was born near Birmingham and one of the Cambridge reformers. In 1534 he was at Antwerp, but on November 25, 1540, he matriculated at Wittenberg, and translated four tracts by Melanchthon during his stay there. He married a Flemish lady and became a Lutheran pastor, and then Superintendent (i.e. Bishop in the Lutheran sense) at Meldorf in Dietmarsch in N.W. Germany. He was known to his friends as a "hearty" person, not in the way of modern muscular evangelicalism, but as one passionate, sincere and eloquent. In the first weeks of Mary's reign he was committed to "house arrest" and in 1555 submitted to a lively series of interrogations before the Chancellor, Stephen Gardiner, an inveterate foe of new Biblical translations. The vivid documents may be read in Foxe, and come to a climax when Gardiner cried out, "No, thou canst prove nothing by the Scripture, the Scripture is dead, it must have a lively expositor." To which Rogers replied, "No, the Scripture is alive!" the great doctrine of the reformers that the Scripture is indeed *autopistos*, self-authenticating, by reason of its truth, and in the inspiration of the Holy Spirit. He was refused permission to communicate with his wife and children and became the protomartyr of the persecution under Mary. He was led out to Smithfield February 4, 1555, where on one side stood his wife, baby at her breast, and at her side the sad retinue of ten children, grouped perhaps like organ pipes, square little un-English faces staring at their father, while on the other side a messenger from the Queen stood with a pardon in case he would recant.

Roger's (Matthew's) Bible follows Tyndale and the Lutheran order and is the last English Bible to have those prefaces and glosses which derive much of their material from Luther himself. It has more notes than any other Bible of the time, upwards of 2,100 of which Mr. Mozley suggests that not more than 10 per cent. can derive from Rogers himself, but which are his gleanings from the best commentaries of the time, Lefèvre, Olivetan, Pellicanus, Munster, Bucer and Tyndale.

At last the King of England's eyes were opening, and it seems that in 1536 a "proceed with caution" signal was given. It resulted in 1538 in the Great Bible, behind which lies the initiative of Thomas Cromwell and Thomas Cranmer and the editorial labour of Coverdale, who went off to Paris where the printing and paper were better than anything available in England. Here it ran foul of the French inquisition, and the stocks were confiscated by the French authorities, though the underground movement was able to rescue four vats of the sheets and to get them safely to England.

The government injunctions of 1538 ordered copies of the English Bible to be set up in the churches and cathedrals of England. The Great Bible was a revision of Coverdale, with the help of versions of Sebastian Münster, Eras-

mus, and the Vulgate. Some of the churches had to make
do with copies of Matthew's Bible until copies of the Great
Bible were available. The church accounts of Great St.
Mary's, Cambridge, show that in Easter 1539 they paid
2s. 6d. for half a Bible (one wonders which half?) and at
Easter 1540, 9s. for half a Bible (the Great Bible was
dearer than that of Coverdale); in 1547 they paid 14s. for a
whole Bible, and in 1562, 13s. 4d.

Stephen Gardiner took the place of More as champion
against the English Bible. Gardiner had begun as a humanist; as a young page in Paris he had buttered lettuce salad
for the great Erasmus, but in later years his motto was, "I
will have no innovation." He roundly attacked Sir John
Cheke and his new pronunciation of Greek, and he intro-
duced into the House of Lords a long list of Latin words
which he said must at all costs be retained in any Scriptures
authorized in English as being exactly rendered, or of
accustomed ecclesiastical usage. We may be thankful to have
been spared many of Gardiner's emendations, which include some horrible Latinisms such as:

"eject the beam out of thine own eye"
"behold the ancille of the Lord"
"this is my dilect son in whom complacui"
"I desire misericord and not sacrifice".

But Gardiner and his friends were not without their
successes in the latter part of the reign of Henry VIII. In
1543 as a result of complaint and criticism the Great Bible
was ordered to be stayed. This was followed by the disastrous and to us ironically entitled Act "for the Advancement
of true religion and for the abolishment of the contrary".
It forbade "all manner of books of the Old and New Testament being of the crafty, false and untrue translation of
Tyndale", and it restricted the reading of the Bible to those
above the rank of artificer. After July 1, it was decreed, "no
women, or artificers, prentices, journeymen, servingmen of
the degrees of yeoman or under, husbandmen or labourers

shall read the Bible or the New Testament in English to himself or any other privately or openly".

Mr. Mozley has a quotation in his fine book on *Coverdale and the English Bibles* which is a most eloquent comment. It is an inscription found in a copy of Langley's *Abridgment of Polydore Vergil*, written by a Gloucestershire shepherd:

> At Oxforde the yere 1546 browt down to Seynbury by John darby pryse-14 d when I kepe Mr Letymers shype I bout this boke when the testament was obberagatyd that shepe herdys might not Red hit, I prey God Amende that blyndnes. wryt by Robert Wyllyams Keppynge shepe upon Seynbury hill 1546.

This comment by a shepherd in the very Tyndale country reminds us how far the Church had removed itself from the daring liberty of a God, who long ago had entrusted his church to fishermen, and who had revealed his son to shepherds keeping their sheep upon the hills of Bethlehem. Against the opening of the Bible there was the argument put forward by Standish in 1540:

> The Universal church of Christ did never approve scripture to be in the vulgar tongue, weighing the manifold inconveniences that have issued therefrom . . . the well must be covered lest the younglings fall into it and so be drowned.

Let us admit they had a case: if men spoke in that age of the open Bible as today we speak of the atomic bomb, we must allow for the terrible casualties when the Bible got into the hands of obscurantists and fanatics, casualties which, it may well be, outnumber those of Nagasaki and Hiroshima. But to concentrate on such perversion as though this was the main consequence of opening the Scriptures to common men is as foolish as to pretend that the marginal glosses were all that mattered in the first English Bibles. In fact the Scriptures were, as Rogers said, alive. They had their own message, they were able to build up men and women in holy living and holy dying. Comparisons are odious and we need not become involved in the vain argument how far the gospel was taught to the common people in the Middle Ages in other ways than by preaching and reading the Word of God. All we need to do is to emphasize that in these ways now, at the Reformation, vehicles of Christian proclamation and instruction were opened which bred their own type of religion and powerfully reconditioned the whole English religious life. The sanctity of George Herbert, so markedly different from that of counter-Reformation piety on the Continent, would not have had its distinctive quality apart from the English Bible and the English Book of Common Prayer. And the same is true of countless millions of ordinary men and women. They found that to humble faith the Scriptures were an open, not a closed book. They would have agreed with Charles Wesley in a quaint verse:

> No matter how dull the scholar whom he
> Takes into his school, he makes him to see.
> A wonderful fashion of teaching he hath,
> And wise to salvation he makes us through faith.

Or, as Tyndale put it in prose of limpid beauty:

> Who taught the eagles to spy out their prey? Even so the children of God spy out their Father: and Christ's elect spy out their Lord and trace out the paths of his feet and follow. Yea, though he be upon the plain and liquid water which will receive no step, and yet there they find out his foot: his elect know him.

The case for the open Bible rests in the end not on an estimate of the intellectual capacities of common men: though I would not deny that the doctrine of Scripture as *autopistos* includes the affirmation of the intrinsic validity of truth and the capacity of men to acknowledge it—the Christianity, that is, of what we shall see is the grand Miltonic argument in *Areopagitica*. But it rests in the main on the fact that the God who made all men and spent himself in their redemption wills by his Spirit to lead men home in a plain way to himself, and that in the end we are not as children to be protected from the adventure of truth, nor slaves who need not be told more than is good for them, but sons of God.

There was a new spirit abroad in the dawn of the Reformation which refused to treat grown men as babies, and which indeed rather treated babes as adults. There is a delightful preface to an edition of Lilly's grammar in 1543 in the name of the young King:

> Ye tender babes of England, shake off slothfulness, set wantonness aside, apply your wits to learning and virtue whereby you much profit yourselves and much advance the common weal of your country. Let noble Prince Edward encourage your tender hearts, a prince of great towardness . . . now almost in readiness to run the same race of learning as yourself.

The Government of Edward VI reckoned with the problems of opening the Bible. From the first the Bible had been read aloud, by the literate to the illiterate, and when the English Bible was chained in churches it was expected that it would not simply be read silently as modern men read newspapers in a public library. But there had already been difficulties. What of the marginal notes? Should they be read? We know that Tyndale's (Luther's) *Preface to the Romans* was included in Matthew's Bible and there was a great rumpus when somebody read it out to a listening group in Calais. There were those who began to expound what they read, and there was a truculent group which refused to cease this exercise when the divine offices began in the choir. There were other ways to bring the Bible home. The sermons of Luther in Germany, and of Latimer in England, with their almost naïve way of re-telling Bible stories familiar to us, but perhaps not so familiar to that generation, remind us, as is well known on the modern

mission field, how fresh and striking the old Bible stories may
be made when they are re-told with devout imagination.
And here the Government of Edward found an invaluable
instrument of Biblical education in the famous "paraphrases
of Erasmus" which were also commanded to be set up and
read in Churches. It is sometimes said that these were
rabidly anti-clerical, and there is a good deal of moralizing
in the Erasmian manner. But the really notable character
of them (and the Princess Mary had a hand in translating
part of them) is their simple re-telling of the Gospel story
with just enough detail to give them something of the
freshness that nowadays we get from a new translation or
paraphrase.

Thus in the story of how Jesus healed the man sick of
the palsy (Mark 2) Erasmus says:

> "The sick man began, not by little and little and at the
> length with much ado to move himself: but as soon as
> Jesus had spoken the word, he raised himself and stood
> up as lusty and courageous as though he had never felt
> any palsy at all. Then lifted he up his bed, and laid it on
> his shoulders, and so went out through the press of the
> people, showing them all a new sight, that had never
> been seen before that day, inasmuch as he who a little
> before bedred and carried like a dead carcass on fewer
> men's shoulders was now cranke and lustie."

Mr. Mozley has pointed out that the Government under
Mary never put out an edict against the Bible, and though
there is ample evidence of English Bibles being destroyed
and confiscated there were many retained, he thinks perhaps
between a third and a half.

Thus Tyndale, Coverdale and Rogers laid a good founda-
tion. I cannot speak now of the other notable Bibles
which preceded the King James Bible: the Geneva Bible
so beloved of the Puritans, the Bishops' Bible put forth by
Archbishop Parker, the Catholic versions of Rheims and
Douai. Butterworth on the basis of a slightly precarious

analysis concludes that 60 per cent of the English Bible had received its literary shape before 1611. He thinks, on the basis of selected passages that

The Wycliffite Bible provides			4	per cent.
,, Tyndale	,,	,,	18	,,
,, Coverdale	,,	,,	13	,,
,, Geneva	,,	,,	19	,,
,, Bishops'	,,	,,	4	,,
,, Other versions		,,	3	,,

Thus, though we cannot weigh such imponderables we can trace the impact of the Bible in all ranks of English society in the 16th century. It came into the Court quite early, as Anne Boleyn's lovely copy of Tyndale's Testament reveals, and it stayed there among the nobility and gentry of the realm: the merchants were not all covetous men only interested in account books: a Humphrey Monmouth and a Richard Hilles pored lovingly over the books they had financed, not merely with an eye to the main chance but with an eye to eternal salvation. In humbler walks of life it was treasured by the Lollards of the Chiltern hills, to whom it came as a new refreshing breeze of inspiration, widening narrowed horizons: hidden in his bed straw by day, it was read at night by the haberdasher's assistant William Maldon and his fellow prentice William Jeffreys, as well as by Robert Williams keeping his flocks upon Saintbury Hill. Amid the fire and earthquake of the 16th-century Reformation let us not ignore the sound of gentle stillness, dropping as the gentle rain from heaven upon the place beneath.

For as the rain cometh down . . . and watereth the earth and maketh it bring forth and bud, and giveth seed to the sower and bread to the eater, so shall my Word be that goeth forth out of my mouth: it shall not return unto me void, but it shall accomplish that which I please and it shall prosper in the thing whereto I send it.

c

CHAPTER II

THOMAS CRANMER AND
THE BOOK OF COMMON PRAYER

IF Thomas Cranmer is, as Lord Houghton said, "the most mysterious personage" in the story of the English Reformation—at least in the front rank—it is partly because, like Luther, he is so bound up with what he did that we tend to judge him as we evaluate the Reformation. Happily, all that may be said against him was said long ago, and by his near contemporaries even more vividly and directly than by the 19th-century historians, from Macaulay, Froude, via the Oxford Movement, to the archivists Brewer, Gairdner and Pocock. There was the priest of Scarborough who said that "he is an hosteler and hath as much learning as the gooslynges upon the grene that goo yonder". Or Harpsfield's description of him as the "Divil's Jackanapes who made pastime to Lucifer and his angels". Or the brutal forthrightness of Dr. Martin at his trial, "there was a compact between you and the King: give me the Archbishopric of Canterbury and I will give you license to live in adultery"; while Foxe reports a milder version of the same slander—"his archiepiscopal dignity of many hath been thought to have been procured by friendship only, and of some others esteemed unworthy of so high vocation".

Yet the truth about him lies also in ancient and primary documents. Important among them are the "Anecdotes" which at the age of 70 his faithful servant Ralph Morice wrote down for Matthew Parker. They are to be read no doubt with discrimination. When he reports conversations made before he entered Cranmer's service, or what the King told Cranmer behind closed doors, we may suspend confidence, but when he tells us how he overheard Cromwell talking with his master at dinner, or how Cranmer, when deeply moved, had a way of biting his lips, we may unreservedly listen. The narratives in Foxe are honest, though he had a habit, borrowed from Thucydides, of filling in gaps in speeches, and sometimes his corroborative details appear to be derived from sources that we wot not of! Two lively Catholic documents give accounts of his last days. The first, Archbishop Cranmer's *Recantacyons*, was re-discovered by Lord Houghton at the end of the 19th century, and like many such "finds" was overvalued by the first historians to use it. The other document is the famous letter, signed "A. J.", written by a Catholic witness of the execution, penned within days of its occurrence.

Thomas Cranmer was born at Aslacton, near Nottingham, in 1489. His schooling was severe and damaged his memory and his spirit. But he was much more of a tough than the phrase "gentle scholar" suggests, and the famous portrait of him suggests one early bred, as he was, to the long bow, one who in mature life could manage the roughest horse in the Canterbury stables, and who as a youth loved hunting, hawking and to shoot the deer with the cross bow. He may have come to Cambridge at the not unusual age of 14, and would have undergone the usual arts courses, the "Trivium" and "Quadrivium". He also had a grounding in the schoolmen and at the end of his life could confute his opponents with a citation from Scotus or Gabriel Biel. It is likely that he turned to the new Biblical theology and the Erasmian tools, the sacred languages, and the study of those editions of the Fathers of East and West which poured from the presses in the first decades of the century and which were the Erasmian antidote to late scholasticism. On the whole, it is perhaps unlikely that he belonged to the famous "White Horse" group of reformers, if this were a coherent closed society, like the Wesley "Holy Club". But there is real evidence of his early concentration on Bible study, and that he was from the first, and unlike the young Martin Luther, an anti-papalist, one who would not accept the canonist doctrines of the papal "plenitude of power".

He became a Fellow of Jesus College, but resigned when, as Morice rather quaintly puts it, "he chanced to marry a wife". It is sure that she lived at the Dolphin inn which stood at the Bridge Street end of All Saints Passage, opposite Jesus Lane. At his trial, when asked whether her name was "Joan Black" or "Joan Brown", Cranmer a little oddly said that he did not remember! In any case, she seems to have been a kinswoman of the owner of the inn, and Cranmer's visits there gave rise to the slander that he was a pub haunter, an "hosteler". The Catholic statement that she was "wont to sell the young scholars their breakfasts" suggests that perhaps we should think of her less in the "non-U" status of barmaid, as in the more "U" category of a modern coffee house waitress.

When she died in childbirth, Cranmer returned from his lecturing in Buckingham College, and resumed his Fellowship at Jesus. In the next years, a little late in life, he read for Holy Orders, and the period left him all his days a scholar and very much a don. The trait comes out almost comically in 1538, when the King sent him the royal comments on the Bishops' Book and got instead such raps over the royal knuckles as suggest that Cranmer had gone back in a reverie to his supervisions, to coping with the ramblings of some precocious and trying adolescent. "This word agreeth not with the three verbs to which it is referred . . . this obscureth the sentence and is superfluous" . . . "the praeter sense may not be joined with the present tense" . . . "this maketh the sentence very dark and ambiguous"—and the unkindest cut of all, "this is well added—and yet there might be said more amply . . ." He remained a friend of his college, and soon after he became Archbishop sent a present of game—"I send you a buck to be bestowed among your company within your college. And forasmuch as you have more store of money, also less need than I at this season, therefore I bequeath a noble of your purse towards the baking and seasoning of him." And in 1535 he intervened swiftly to stop one of Thomas Cromwell's felonious little plans which had to do with the college property, while it may well be that it was college business which first brought him into contact with the Court of Henry VIII.

Suddenly this "remote and ineffectual don" was snatched into the world of affairs, the immense reverberation of the King's "great cause", the royal divorce. In the summer of 1529 Cranmer had retired before the plague at Cambridge and was staying with two pupils, distant kinsmen, at Waltham. There unexpectedly came the King, in the critical days after his case had been so disconcertingly revoked to Rome. Two of Wolsey's brightest young men, Edward Foxe and Stephen Gardiner, one Provost of King's and the other Master of Trinity Hall, rising diplomats, had a long talk with Cranmer. What they said is not, I think, as clear as some of the history books make out, but it was important enough for them to report their conversation to the King, and the upshot was that Cranmer was lodged in London. There he drew up a learned writing, marshalling a body of evidence, Biblical, patristic, and conciliar and scholastic, to show that for a man to marry his brother's wife (as Henry had married Katherine) was contrary to divine law and law natural, and so indispensable even by the Papal plenitude of power. What became of the book is a mystery, though it may be among the Cotton MSS, and it is my guess we may read its arguments in their refutation by Harpsfield in the first book of his "Pretended Divorce of Henry VIII" (ed. Camden Society). The book was immediately used by Foxe and Gardiner to win over the strong body of adverse opinion in the Divinity Faculty at Cambridge, where in February 1530 Foxe and Gardiner used such tactics as sailed near the wind of honesty. Cranmer himself was by this time abroad and he was sent to present his arguments at Rome itself, as part of an embassy headed by Anne Boleyn's father, the Earl of Wiltshire.

A year later he went himself as ambassador to the Emperor, and saw something at first hand of the horrors of 16th-century warfare. Perhaps the sight struck home, for later, when he was Archbishop at Canterbury, and the disabled soldiers came hobbling home from the French wars, he turned one of his Kentish manors into a hospital, and provided for them nurses, doctors, medicine, and paid their fares home. In the city of Nuremberg he watched with eager interest the liturgical experiments there, and his companion, Sir Thomas Eliot, wrote home:

> Mr. Cranmer sayeth it was showed him that in the Epistles and Gospels they kept not the order that we do, but peruse every day a chapter of the New Testament.

Here he made friends with the Nuremberg reformer Andrew Osiander, who found Cranmer's interest in his many books flattering, until he found that the English scholar was even more interested in his niece Margaret, whom he now married. This is, among other things, evidence of the strength of Cranmer's reforming convictions at this time. A few weeks before, in Cambridge, Nicholas Shaxton, a future master of Gonville Hall, had been brought before the Vice-Chancellor for saying in an Ash Wednesday sermon in Great St. Mary's that he prayed daily that wedlock might be permitted to the clergy, and he had been constrained to renounce the opinion in order to avoid a public abjuration. It is possible that Cranmer's courting sheds light on his ambassadorial duties. For Duke John Frederick of Saxony, on his way home from Regensburg, was startled when the English ambassador, Thomas Cranmer arrived in Nuremberg in July 1532 and demanded a secret audience, which was given him before the chancellor Brück and his secretary, George Spalatin. They discussed such matters as the Turkish war and their common attitude to the Archduke Ferdinand. Then, a week later, Cranmer turned up in Nuremberg again, with the extraordinary plea that he had forgotten the most important part of his instructions. This time he saw Spalatin alone, and according to the Weimar archives he opened up the possibility of Henry joining an alliance of German princes against the Habsburgs. We may wonder whether this was the real reason for these repeated trips to the city of Margaret Osiander, and whether the conversation with Spalatin, who had long hesitated about his own marriage, was entirely on diplomatic lines? At least in 1538, when Spalatin had long retired from active Court politics, Cranmer seems to have sent him a handsome present, which may have its origin in a human rather than a political situation!

For Cranmer his marriage was an entirely honourable estate, of which he never repented and had no need to be ashamed. It is true that in the time of the Six Articles he could not publicly avow a union which was in any case known to all the Court. To this period belongs the most famous Cranmer story, how—

> He kept his woman very close, and sometime carried her about with him in a great chest full of holes, that his pretty nobsey might take breath at.

The evidence for this turns out to be a rather tall tale of a fire at Canterbury, when Cranmer showed great anxiety as they took a large crate from the burning building, crying out that "his evidences and other writings which he esteemed above any worldly treasure were in the chest". Which seems to prove no more than that there are, after all, two kinds of scholars: those who treat their wives like a box of books, and those who treat books as though they were their wives— "above any worldly treasure"—and that Cranmer belonged to the second class. The ribald story of Sanders that an ignorant porter tipped the crate on end and left the second Mrs. Cranmer upside down is, a little sadly, completely exploded.

The first moves of the English Reformation were those

of Warham, Cromwell, and the Reformation Parliament. When, in 1532, Cranmer was summoned home to be Archbishop of Canterbury, he delayed his return for many weeks in hope that Henry VIII might change his mind. His *nolo episcopari* is not to be doubted, for none could relish such an office at such a time, even if he dared not add the evangelical excuse, "I have married a wife . . ."

That Thomas Cranmer, and not Stephen Gardiner should have been chosen as Primate is matter for reflection. Perhaps Henry did not want a strong, dominating figure who might be yet another turbulent priest. For Cranmer, amiable and impressive as his presence was, was no party leader, not perhaps a leader of men at all, and in a crisis would make his protest quietly and firmly and then retire to his study or his diocese. But the temper of this gentleness is not to be exaggerated. Nobody has a finer or longer record of courageous intercession with a Henry who in a rage could out-Herod Herod. He interceded for More and Fisher, for the monks of Canterbury, for the Duke of Norfolk and for the Princess Mary. When Anne Boleyn so swiftly fell he wrote the King:

"My mind is clean mazed . . . for I had never better opinion in woman than I had in her . . . your Grace knoweth that next unto your Grace I was most bound to her of all creatures living."

About Thomas Cromwell he was almost reckless:

"Such a servant, in my judgment, in wisdom, diligence, faithfulness and experience, as no prince in this realm ever had . . . if the noble princes of memory, King John(!), Henry the Second, and Richard III (!), had such a councillor about them I suppose that they should never have been so traitorously abandoned."

It was Cranmer whom the scared Council sent to tax Catherine Howard with her infidelities (where there could be no mercy, since a Queen's adultery involved that "diversity of titles" which lay behind the Wars of the Roses and is among the shadows behind all Henry's matrimonial affairs). And when he left her amid a frenzied shock of hysteria and fear, he had to break the news to Henry himself, whom grief and rage turned into a tormented animal.

Historians, a little belatedly, now take seriously Cranmer's doctrine of the "Godly Prince". When at his consecration he made public protest, in Chapter House and at the altar, that he took his vows of obedience to the Pope subject to the laws of England, and that he did not intend to "disable myself . . . any way concerning the Reformation of Christian religion, the government of the Church of England, or the prerogatives of the Crown thereof", it may partly have been that had he not done so the threat of *Praemunire* so recently stretched beyond all previous extension might have hung over his later actions, but it was much more the honest scruple of firm conviction, his belief in the supremacy of the Godly Prince, as in 1540 he classically expounded the notion:

> "All Christian Princes have committed unto them immediately of God, the whole cure of all their subjects, as well concerning the administration of God's word for the cure of souls, as concerning the ministration of things political, and civil governance."

In the relation between Cranmer and his King there was more than ideology—on Cranmer's side respect for an element of greatness in Henry almost hidden from our eyes, but which Cardinal Pole also saw. And in his later years, when Henry trusted hardly anybody, he gave him his confidence. "After dinner", says Ralph Morice, "I heard my lord Cromwell say to my lord Cranmer. You were born in a happy hour, I suppose for do or say what you will, the King will take it at your hand." The story, made famous by Shakespeare, how the Council plot to send Cranmer to the Tower was foiled because the King had given him a signet ring, seems to be true. For it is Morice who tells how they kept Cranmer kicking his heels among the lackeys, and it was Morice who fetched Dr. Butts, the royal physician, who indignantly told the King. And it is Morice, as well as Shakespeare, who tells how at the critical moment Cranmer confounded his enemies by producing the ring, and how Henry made each member apologize in turn.

It was Cromwell, not Cranmer, who as royal Vice-Gerent carried through the Dissolution of the Monasteries. But two creative works belong also to Henry's reign. The first, the English Bible, and if it is to Thomas Cromwell that we owe its official promulgation, Cranmer's heart was in the business too, and he wrote to Cromwell, "you have shown me more pleasure therein than if you had given me a thousand pounds".

In 1544 came Cranmer's own liturgical first-fruits, the English Litany, revealing what Charles Williams calls his mastery of the "matchless beauty of the shapèd syllable". In a letter to the King he confessed:

"I have . . used more than the liberty of a translator: for in some processions I have altered diverse words: in some I have added part: in some taken part away—some I have left out whole . . . in mine opinion the song to be made thereto would not be full of notes, but as near as may be, for every syllable a note . . . . I have travailed to make verses in English . . . only for a proof to see how English would do in song. But because mine English verses lack the grace and facility which I wish they had your majesty may cause some other to make them again."

He was, alas, and unlike Luther, no musician or singing man, and apart from his version of "Salve festa dies" the great mediaeval hymns had to wait for John Mason Neale. To describe Cranmer's Litany as a lovely service would indeed be rather like describing the Day of Judgment as a pretty sight, but it has always been recognized as a noble, worthy vehicle of solemn intercession.

Among the manuscripts in the British Museum is a

document which in modern times has been re-published by Dr. Wickham Legg as *Cranmer's Liturgical Projects*. It is a fascinating document, for in it we can watch the gestation of one of Cranmer's liturgical marvels. The divine offices had become too complicated and badly needed pruning. There was need to restore the regular rotation of Psalms and Scripture reading, so that the Psalms were to be read once a month, the Bible once a year, rather like a good running clock where the Psalms, the minute hand, go round quickly within the slower pattern of the hours, the Scripture. The *Projects* show us two stages in the great creative work of turning the seven Latin choir offices into the two English congregational services of Mattins and Evensong. The document has two preliminary schemes bound together: a conservative Latin version of the seven offices, and a more radical Latin form for Mattins and Evensong. Despite the persuasive voices of Charles Smyth and Professor Ratcliffe I think there are sound reasons for supposing that Cranmer began with the more conservative experiment, akin to the reforms of the Cardinal Quiñon, and went on to the more drastic anticipation of his vernacular services. But it is not his originality which is decisive. The Primers, Thomas Müntzer, and the Strasbourg liturgies had all preceded him with vernacular Mattins and Evensongs, but it is the quality of the new shape which made them into a normative pattern of English devotion. In the "Festivale" and the "Sanctorale" at the end of the MS of the *Projects*, which at this point seem to have been rather misunderstood, there is evidence that Cranmer toyed with the idea of reformed "fourth lessons", i.e. non-scriptural readings about the saints, but that these were to be no longer doubtful fables from the "Golden Legend" but reputable stories from the patristic writings of East and West, pointing evangelical truths. And we may wonder whether in dropping the scheme something did not go out of English devotion which was not to be recovered until the Caroline divines, perhaps not until the Oxford Movement.

It is to Edward's reign that his greatest works belong. He was chief architect of the Prayer Books (which does not mean that everything good or bad in them is necessarily his, and I have a feeling that Charles Smyth may be right when he says that Cranmer's real heart was in the first rather than the second Book): he was chief author of the classic Homily of Salvation (with its lucid, balanced exposition of *sola fide*) of the articles of faith, and of the scheme for the reform of Canon Law.

Of his drastic revision of the ancient liturgy in the Communion service, and at the point of the Canon, two simple comments may be made.

Like Luther, also a conservative liturgist, Cranmer believed it was needful to return the eucharist to the form of a Communion of the faithful. He further believed that the abuses concerning the sacrifice of the Mass, and much current exposition of its doctrine, demanded a surgical, major operation on the older service. Modern Roman teaching about the eucharistic sacrifice is so remote from that of such 16th-century Romanists as Ambrosius Catherinus that we may easily miss the need for his immense insistence on the once-for-all-ness of the Cross:

> He made there by his one oblation of himself once offered a full, perfect and sufficient sacrifice, oblation and satisfaction for the sins of the whole world.

There is nothing quite as emphatic as this, I think, in any Protestant liturgy of the Reformation. It is perhaps no accident that the only lectures of Cranmer of which we know are those which he gave to his clergy one Lent on the Epistle to the Hebrews. I think we may find echoes of them in the fifth book of his great eucharistic treatise against Stephen Gardiner, and those who turn to it will find how rich and positive, and scriptural, is his doctrine.

Second, Cranmer's own conversion from a traditional belief in the Real Presence of Christ according to his humanity, to what we may call a True Presence, was of deep personal importance to him, so that in the last months of his life it was almost an obsession with him to defend his doctrine, to finish his argument against Gardiner, even though his old opponent was dead. I think we do well to be chary of labels in this matter, for the differences between the radicals who denied the Lutheran and Roman doctrines were many, and the issues complex, and in the main stresses of Cranmer's doctrine he goes in some places beyond Bucer, who used the realistic language of the Fathers to convey a doctrine of a true spiritual presence, and who, if we may say so, was on the right hand of the left wing of the Protestant reformers.

Behind all this work there is deep scholarship. His own private collection of books is said to have outnumbered the university library and the record of some 350 has survived, out of all learning of East and West, Fathers and Schoolmen, liturgists and exegetes. He had not the best physical equipment for a great divine: he was short-sighted and his memory was bad, but he and his secretaries distilled this learning into great commonplace books, and their lore underpins the homily of Justification and the exposition of eucharistic doctrine.

He was a slow reader, but a diligent marker of whatsoever he read, for he seldom read without a pen in his hand, and whatsoever made for either the one part or the other of things being in controversy, he wrote it out if it were short, or at the least noted the author of it.

That is perhaps why he does not seem to have made many new prayers, though he may perhaps have created the noble "Prayer of Humble Access", of which there is an echo in his prayer before his execution. His learning and his conservatism gave him flexibility. He could combine old mediaeval liturgy with new Reformation rite, to make something new, or with what looks at first sight almost a verbal twist, could take a few sentences from the rather banal order of Cologne, and give us of a sudden the unforgettable

"Comfortable Words". Such things did Thomas Cranmer with his right hand, and though Professor Ratcliffe has shown that Cranmer ranged less widely than some liturgists have supposed, his great authority sums up the matter—"whatever the defects of his two Prayer Books, Cranmer's liturgical achievement, considered against the limitations which beset him, is nothing short of the prodigious".

He collected books. In 1548, a dangerous hour in Protestant history, he collected scholars also, for he offered asylum in these islands to a grateful band of polyglot divines, and dreamed to make these islands the scene of a truly, free Christian council. Peter Martyr, Ochino, Bucer, Fagius, A. Lasco, Poullain and a whole company of lesser lights, scholars and students and their families. He did what he could for them all.

In the last months of the reign of Edward, Cranmer was in great disfavour with Northumberland and his Government. At a time when England toppled on the verge of such catastrophe as was to beset Scotland and France, where the Crown became the tug of war between warring noble factions, Cranmer resisted where he could, refusing to impeach his old adversary Cuthbert Tunstall, protesting against the spoliation of the churches, while at the end he resisted to the last the desperate ploy of Queen Jane. Then came that dreadful last interview with his dying Prince, a boy of fifteen years, who had not eaten for days, drugged, propped on pillows, gaunt of face, with frightened eyes, discussing what was to happen after his own funeral—no wonder if at last Cranmer yielded to the petulent question of his godly prince whether he alone would withstand the royal will. And so Cranmer signed after, but with the rest of the council, and when he did so, as he said, he signed unfeignedly and without dissimulation.

It meant that when Mary rode in triumph into London Cranmer, too, had fallen into treason, and he began characteristically to sell his plate and settle his debts, that when he died he might owe no man anything. There was some talk that he might be allowed to retire on a pension into private life, and in a letter to the Queen he seems to have been willing to do so.

> It lieth not in me, but in your grace only, to see reformation of things that be amiss. To private subjects it appertaineth not to reform things, but quietly to suffer that they cannot amend.

But when the slander circulated that he had ordered Mass to be said in Canterbury he was roused to a more heroic sense of responsibility. He wrote what began as a denial and ended as a manifesto, offering publicly to defend the doctrine and shape of the Prayer Book. And though it was against his will and without his knowledge that this was copied and circulated, he himself, he told the council, had intended to have it affixed to the door of St. Paul's and other London churches, with his seals affixed. So he went to join Latimer and Ridley in the Tower.

For a time their lives were safe: England was not reconciled with Rome, and the Heresy Acts had been repealed. In 1555 they were removed to Oxford and there disputed on the eucharist. But it seems that, for reasons of policy, Cranmer was treated with more deference than Latimer or Ridley. At least he was allowed to act as interlocutor in a D.D. disputation which his restraint and learning turned into a personal triumph, so that at the end the regent of debate said:

> "Your wonderful gentle behaviour and modesty, Master D. Cranmer, is worthy much commendation . . . . I give you most hearty thanks in mine own name, and in the name of all my brethren."

At which saying all the doctors gently put off their caps.

He was not at the window of Bocardo prison when Ridley and Latimer were led out to die: but he seems to have watched their burning from the roof and if so, the dreadful dying of Ridley, whose fire was ill made and who leaped about shrieking "I cannot burn!" must have remained as a searing memory during the following months when Cranmer's company before was gone, and he remained alone. For Cranmer's case lay with the Pope, who appointed the Prefect of the Inquisition in Rome to proceed in his name, and who named Brookes, Bishop of Gloucester, to be his commissioner. On September 12, 1556, Cranmer appeared before him in St. Mary's Church and Brookes made a very moderate oration, encouraging Cranmer to hope that by submission and recantation he might yet save his life and station. "We come not to judge you: but to put you in remembrance of that you have been, and shall be. . . ." "And whereas you were Archbishop of Canterbury and metropolitan of England, it is ten to one (I say) that ye shall be as well still, yea, and rather better."

Cranmer was then cited to appear before the Pope in Rome within eighty days, and when he did not, being kept in prison, he was declared contumacious and the order followed for his formal degradation. The ritual for degrading an Archbishop is curious, and involves a marvellous quantity of paraphernalia. For the Archbishop is first vested in a canvas parody of his pontificals and made to hold a dummy crozier, and is then divested of each rank of his seven orders in turn, while at each stage the instruments of his order (as, for the priesthood the chalice) are given him and then snatched from his hands. The solemn foolery went on with a mixture of high tragedy and bathos. Bishop Bonner made an extravagantly rhetorical, silly speech so venomous that his fellow commissioner plucked his sleeve and begged him to desist. For his fellow was Thirleby of Ely, a friend of Cranmer from his undergraduate days, upon whom Cranmer had showered such benefits that, as he tried in mime to scrape the anointed oil from Cranmer's fingers, his choking sobs drowned all the voices in the Church. In the main, Cranmer submitted, though when they took his pall he cried out "Which of you hath a pall to take away mine?" and when the barber stepped forward to shave his head, Cranmer, who had been quite bald since the days of Henry VIII, said "I had done with all this gear long ago!" And when at last he stood unfrocked, dressed in the clothes of a poor bargeman—*in servitutem et ignominiam habitus*—Bonner cried out, "Now are you Lord no more." Cranmer once said that he "never set more by any title, name or style, that I write than by the paring of an apple", but he must have deeply felt this humiliation. While we may, if we will, reflect that this after all was a rather Protestant service, since its object was to erase what on Catholic principles might be supposed to be indelible. And we may wonder whether even the Quakers ever put a more ironic question mark against Ecclesiastical Man than the fact that when all the layers had been removed, an Archbishop had been at last revealed "in the FORM OF A SERVANT" —i.e. in the only holy garments ever assumed by the Lord and Maker of the Church.

At the degradation he had handed to Thirleby an appeal to a General Council, drawn up for him by a lawyer friend, and intended, he said, to enable him to gain time, a respite in which to finish a book against his old antagonist Stephen Gardiner, who was now dead but who lived on in a eucharistic treatise under the name of Marcus Antonius Constantinus. But in it Cranmer hinted that he would be willing to listen to instruction, and this I believe was the beginning of his failure of nerve. It is notable that the two finest scholars of the Cambridge Reformation, Sir John Cheke and Thomas Cranmer, were both induced to sign an ascending series of documents each more compromising than the last. As a technique, modern enough. But those in charge of Cranmer, Spanish friars and Oxford dons, did not in the best modern manner put Cranmer in a black hole, or in the glare of an electric light: they neither beat him up nor starved him. They were more clever, and perhaps more cruel. He was suddenly taken from Bocardo and lodged in the guest room of the Dean of Christ Church: and they dined him, and he walked on the lawns and played bowls with the Fellows, back unbelievably in that world he had left at Jesus

D

thirty years before. And he signed this time a real, formal, witnessed recantation. We may believe the men at Oxford meant him well: they really hoped that this might save his life. It was away in London that three implacable wills were determined on his death: Mary, Philip and the Cardinal Pole. They sent down, by the hands of the Provost of Eton, the writ for his burning, and another form of recantation, a horrible and abject grovel in which he took blame for all the evil in the land in the last twenty years, and announced himself the vilest man on earth. Perhaps this document, cruel and humiliating beyond measure, did more than anything to bring Cranmer to his senses. But what it failed to do was achieved when he learned that despite his recantation he was still to die. There was no longer uncertainty to confuse the mind. The Pope and the Queen failed with him in the end because they overreached themselves and allowed the case to be revoked before a higher tribunal, the conscience when a man confronts the living God, in the dread article of death. In the margin of Sir John Cheke's recantations Matthew Parker wrote the kindly comment, "Homines sumus" ("We are only men, after all"). But conscience, says S. T. Coleridge, "makes heroes of us all". And so Thomas Cranmer died a martyr.

What this prospect of death means to a church leader is remote from the experience of most of us. But Bishop Berggrav of Norway has written of his own experiences in the modern Church struggle, and shows us what we might have guessed, that face to face with death there is neither archbishop nor bishop, cleric or layman, but only the liberty of a Christian man.

"A Solicitor appeared in my cell", he said, "to tell me that it was decided that I should be shot on Monday. An arrow went through my heart of course, but once again I felt my safeguardedness in God, and when two days later the solicitor reappeared to tell me that the decision had to be altered I almost felt disappointed . . .

so it was all the time . . . half your soul in an anxiety of fear and doubt: the other half of your soul is in heaven, carried on the wings of faith which God bestows on you."

So it may have been with Cranmer. Saturday, March 21, 1556, was wet and blustery and the service set for the execution was diverted to the church of St. Mary the Virgin. There the Provost of Eton preached while Cranmer stood opposite the crowded congregation and wept bitterly. They had drawn up a statement for him to read at the stake, though I think he had a hand in its making, as when he got to its peroration, he suddenly left his notes:

And now I come to the great thing which troubleth my conscience more than any thing that I ever did or said in my whole life, and that is, the setting abroad of a writing contrary to the truth, which now here I renounce and refuse, as things contrary to the truth, which I thought in my heart, and have written for fear of death, and to save my life, if it might be and that is such bills and papers as I have written or signed with my hand since my degradation . . . and forasmuch as my hand . . . hath offended contrary to my heart, my hand shall first be punished, for may I come to the fire, it shall first be burned. And as for the Pope I refuse him as Christ's enemy and Anti-Christ, with his false doctrine. And as for the Sacrament. . . ."

He got no further: the stunned silence broke into uproar and confusion above which the secular arm, Lord Williams, cried out "Have you gone mad?" They plucked him down, but he strode before them so that his guardian friars must run to keep pace with him, in their pleading. He was deathly white—*exalbescit*, say the account, and the dying thieves in Peter Breughel's great "Crucifixion" are the best comment on that chalky whiteness. No historian believes it, but the early Catholic account says that he cried at the stake, "Now I see the heavens open and Jesus Christ standing at the right hand of God." His own right hand he thrust into the fire and he kept it there, save once to wipe his face, until the end. "His patience in torment", wrote a hostile eye witness, "his courage in dying, if it had been for the glory of God . . . I could worthily have commended his example, and matched it with the fame of any Father of ancient time."

He had contrived the impossible: a deed which out-matched even the last noble words of Latimer to Ridley. His death is the watershed in the reign of Mary, a turning-point in the story of the English Reformation. We who go, four hundred years after, "the holy blisful martir for to seek", know where to look for his memorial. It lies not in some bedecked shrine in his great cathedral, but in that other fabric, not made with hands but not less real, and not without its jewels, of which the liturgy is but the outward frame. That was no mean workmanship, quarried from many sources, yet fitly framed together which through four centuries bore, as it still bears, the heavy burden of a people's prayers.

CHAPTER III

JOHN FOXE AND HIS "BOOK OF MARTYRS"

THE English Bible and the Book of Common Prayer still live, powerfully affecting the spirits of millions of people. Now we have to speak of another great normative document, which also laid its imprint on the English Protestant tradition but which is no longer alive. Foxe's *Book of Martyrs* was accorded the solemn dignity of being bought and chained in the churches of England, and well on in the 19th century Lord Macaulay told how

> as a child he sat of a Sunday afternoon longing to get at the great black letter volume of the Book of Martyrs, which was chained to the neighboring reading desk.

The sturdily Protestant homes of Victorian England gave it, along with *Pilgrim's Progress*, its last burst of popularity, and it was considered fit reading for Sunday when other books were shut away. Some years ago an old lady gave me three folio volumes of the book, and told me in a letter how she and her brothers used to sit in the study of a Kentish rectory on Sunday afternoons while her father read aloud to them from Foxe, and while her eldest brother, as a special privilege, was allowed to curl up in a corner with a folio volume to himself. And as I leafed through the long-neglected pages there fell out a slim yellow-backed paper with the title *Adventures of Sixteen String Jack*, and I wondered if this, too, were not a comment on Victorian religion, and on the kind of literary competition which has relegated the *Book of Martyrs* to the antiquarians.

The Protestantism of Kingsley's *Westward Ho!* is a kind

of pre-Raphaelite view of Elizabeth's day, but there is a real pedigree between them. One of the fruits of the great Oxford Movement was that it sharply criticized this older Protestantism, and began a reaction which has gone pretty far in our own day and is still rather fashionable in the literary world. Protestantism was ripe for debunking. The attack on Foxe came in a series of learned articles by S. R. Maitland, the librarian of Lambeth Palace, who attacked the integrity, truthfulness and reliability of Foxe. Like Denifle's famous attacks on Luther at the end of the 19th century, it had a great initial success and broke a few stained-glass windows. Complacent and uncritical Protestants had to admit the blemishes in Foxe's work. And if the total amount of successful denigration was not large, the attack certainly exposed a good deal of slovenliness among 19th-century editors of Foxe, who made a badly bungled job of the defence. The anti-Foxe tradition once launched had a long run, especially since it chimed with the prejudices of such archivists and historians as J. S. Brewer and James Gairdner. Only the great High Anglican historian R. W. Dixon kept his head and appreciated the value and integrity of the author. In 1940 a careful and valuable study by Mr. J. F. Mozley may be said to have begun the needful "rebunking" (to coin a needed word) of John Foxe and his book.

John Foxe (1517–87) was born at Boston in Lincolnshire, and while he was young his father died and it fell to his stepfather, Richard Melton to see to his schooling. He was rather a lonely, devout boy (to be found at his prayers in church or deep in a book when his friends were at play), and this intensity was a life-long trait. It seems that a certain John Hawarden or Harding of Brasenose College, Oxford, became his patron, and he was able to enter Magdalen college in 1534 (B.A. 1537, M.A. 1543), becoming a Fellow in 1539, a teacher of logic, and in his own studies one deeply learned in the Fathers and the linguistic tongues, a master of Latin which he wrote well, and able to use Hebrew—in short, a humanist of the Indian summer of humanism which flourished in the 1540s in England and of which the fine flower was the scholarship of Sir Thomas Smith and Sir John Cheke.

But John Foxe was a "gospeller" and also a "character" whose oddities become the butt of college gossip, and in this, the period following the Six Articles of 1539, he had dangerous observers. His absence from Mass and from college devotions did not pass unremarked, particularly when he was observed sighing and groaning within himself, pacing o' nights beneath the trees in the grove outside the college.

In 1544 he appealed to the President of Magdalen against his enemies who, he says, had been attacking him these five years, and his defence, though spirited, leaves some things unexplained:

> They say I did not hear Mass, did not go to church . . . yet I was present elsewhere. . . . They say I was studying during chapel time. Sometimes certainly, but I was studying the scripture. But I was absent from Mattins: yes, but by permission of the President. But I often came late. This I own was a fault in a healthy mind but not a sick one as mine was. But they say I laughed in church. I allow this to be a fault even in a young man, but it is not a crime.

But Foxe and his evangelical friends Crowley and Cooper were far outnumbered, and in 1545–6 he and six other Fellows resigned and left the college. Throughout his long life Foxe lived on the margin of poverty, and after an interval in the household of William Lucy of Stratford-on-Avon, where he married one Agnes Randall, he came to London, penniless and with a wife to keep. His son tells how one day he was sitting in the noisy, swirling, gossiping company in the nave of St. Paul's

> spent with long fasting, his countenance thin and his eyes hollow, after the ghastly manner of dying men . . .

when there came to him one whom he never remembered seeing before who sitting down by him and saluting him with much familiarity, thrust an untold sum of money into his hand bidding him be of good cheer, adding withal that he knew not how great the misfortunes were which oppressed him, but supposed it was no light calamity: that he should therefore accept in good part that small gift from his countrymen which courtesy had forced him to offer: that he should go and take care of himself and take all occasions to prolong his life: adding that within a few days new hopes were at hand and a more certain condition of livelihood.

And sure enough, he was suddenly entrusted with the care and education of the children of the greatest family in England, next the Royal House. They were the children of that curious Renaissance bravo the Earl of Surrey: minor poet but often in the police court for assault and battery, and quite possibly mad, since after his arrest for going with friends through the streets of London at night, armed with cross bows, with which they launched stones through the windows of such prominent citizens as Sir Thomas Gresham's house, he made the extraordinary defence, that he was not drunk as the council might suppose but:

"My motive was a religious one: though I confess it lies open to misconception. It grieved me, Lords, to see the licentious lives of the citizens of London ... was I to suffer these men to perish without warning? . . . I therefore went at midnight through the streets and shot from my cross bow at their windows, that the stones passing noiselessly through the air, and breaking in suddenly upon their guilty secrecy, might remind them of that punishment which the scriptures tell us Divine justice will inflict on impenitent sinners."

In 1546, with incredible but typical folly, he put the Royal quarterings of Edward the Confessor on his coat-of-arms—a genealogical impudence which touched Henry at his rawest spot, the "diversity of titles" to the throne, and Surrey and his father, the Duke of Norfolk, were arrested for high treason, thrown into the tower, Surrey being executed on Tower Hill in January 1547.

Foxe taught the three eldest children, and one of them, Thomas, became Duke of Norfolk. Long after, when his pupil was disastrously entangled in a plot to wed him to Mary Queen of Scots, Foxe wrote him an earnest, warning letter:

> I beseech you therefore for God's sake be circumspect, and mark well what they be that set you on this work. Examples you have enough within the compass of your own days, whereby you may learn what noble men have been cast away by them, whom they seemed most to trust. Remember I pray you the ensample of Mephiboseth whereof I told you being young.

In June 1550 Foxe was ordained deacon by Ridley, in St. Paul's Cathedral on the first occasion when the new English ordinal was used. At that time he was living with the Duchess of Suffolk, who was a very "grande dame" indeed and a great champion of Protestants, though it is only a fable that she had a dog which she dressed in a rochet and called Stephen Gardiner after the enemy of the Protestants, the Bishop of Winchester.

He had begun to write, like so many younger scholars then and since, beginning by translating sermons of Luther, Oecolampadius and Urbanus Rhegius, then one or two tracts of his own making, on the need for ecclesiastical discipline, but also, and as we shall see, characteristically a plea that the death penalty be not enforced for the sin of adultery.

Then came the reign of Mary, and Foxe after an adventurous journey to the coast made his way, as did several hundred exiles, to Germany, to the Rhineland and to Switzerland. The notion that this exile was a cleverly planned conspiracy of opponents of Mary's régime is a wild surmise of Dr. Garrett's with more facts against it than for it. The exiles went where one would expect them to go—the humanists and lay gentry to Italy, the scholars to the great theologians of Zürich and Geneva, the rest where they could find safe haven and the protection of a kindly disposed Government. The quarrels among the leaders, the financial troubles of some of the most scholarly, and above all the fact that when Elizabeth came to the throne they came back not in one or two coherent parties with a programme and an ultimatum, but curiously haphazardly in ones and twos—all these and other facts suggest that what organization existed, was not prefabricated and not very good.

At any rate, Foxe in exile had a lean and a hard time. He went to Frankfurt, where he found himself willy nilly involved in the liturgical disputes among the exiles, that fantastic affray of Knox and Cox which engendered much heat, volumes of sound, and withal a little light, since what was in question was the first discordant note of a theme which was to be played out in England for the next century, the issue of whether Englishmen should have as Bishop Cox claimed "the face of an English Church", or a further reform of reformation according to the pattern of Geneva and the godly discipline of Calvin or Bullinger. Foxe couldn't help being involved, but he was no violent partisan, and he complained how—

> Even youths, yea, boys of seven years joined in the fray: and the most violent fighters were the aged theologians.

Finally Foxe took himself off to Basle, where he did what many an impecunious scholar did in the 16th century, found employment with a printer at the drudgery of proof reading, and Foxe found such lodgment with the printer Oporinus, for which he had only his room, and bread and water, if Strype is to be trusted in the matter.

Though he was wretchedly poor and often sick, he got on with his own work, and in 1556 wrote a curious religious drama in Latin verse, *Christus Triumphans*, describing the fortunes of the Church from Adam to the Second Coming, where in addition to Biblical characters there appear Psyche, or the soul of the Church, and Pseudamnus or Anti-Christ, a work evidently not in the T. S. Eliot, Christopher Fry class, for it was little regarded though it was translated into French in 1562 and reprinted in London in 1672 as a school textbook, as one of the minor horrors of the 17th-century agreed syllabus. He also produced a simplified scheme of Latin grammar which was so much more complicated than anything before it that it too, was speedily forgotten. And he nearly killed himself trying to translate into Latin the unwieldy second volume of Cranmer's great eucharistic treatise against Gardiner. But by now a more absorbing theme had gripped his time and his attention, the histories of the Martyrs, and at these he laboured in season and out of season, with no secretarial help, for the rest of his life, beginning in 1552 and then on until the last months of his life when, all virtue drained out of him, he lived on a withered old man, from whose shrivelled gloom cheerfulness and thoughtful kindness kept on breaking out.

He returned to England on the death of Mary and found grateful lodgment for ten years in the house of Thomas, Duke of Norfolk, who was perhaps the more eager to show his gratitude to an old teacher, now famous, because he had done little for him in the dangerous interval of Mary's reign. But though Foxe was friendly with all the notables of the Church and *persona grata* with great Gloriana herself, he was still very much the odd man out, and perhaps it was more than the matter of vestments which resulted in his only getting the prebend of Shipton, and for a few months a prebend at Durham which he soon resigned.

He was, as we said, a "character", the kind of person of whom stories went the rounds, never returning to their hearers void. But even at our most critical and sceptical we have to face the evidence that this kind of story was told about him. There was first his generosity, which was as constant as his poverty and must have often been the despair of his wife (and indeed parsons' wives generally find this a problem with which to cope). He not only gave away his own money but that of his merchant friends, so that there came to him from every quarter deserving beggars and impostors. There is the story of how he left the house of his friend Aylmer, Bishop of London and found the poor waiting for him, so went back and borrowed five pounds which he bestowed cheerfully and graciously and then completely forgot. Some months later the Bishop reminded his friend of the money. "Oh", said Foxe, "I have laid it out for you and have paid it where you owed it, to the poor people that lay at your gate." The Bishop no doubt with a nice irony thanked him for being so careful a steward.

Then there were his prayers, and his devotion which was a byword, prayers with a strangely prophetic quality such that people came to attribute to him a gift of healing and of second sight. And it seems that there were cases of mental illness which he really did cure and which in these days of mental healing we need not doubt as did the liberal historians of the 19th century, and which led his sons (one of whom became a distinguished President of the College of Physicians) to put on his epitaph among other things the word *thaumaturgus*.

Then there were enough stories about his second sight to support what is now quite fashionably referred to in intellectual academic circles as ESP (extra-sensory perception). There is the famous story of how he suddenly cried out at the time of the Spanish Armada in 1588, "They are gone! They are gone!" and so announced for the first time the destruction of the Armada. Unfortunately the story has difficulties, among them the fact that in 1588 Foxe had been dead a year! But if that story is not true, it is quite certain that Sir Francis Drake wrought the destruction of the original Armada in 1587, as he thought, not without the aid of Foxe. For his letter has survived:

> Master Foxe, whereas we have had of late such happy success against the Spaniards, I do assure myself you have faithfully remembered us in your good prayers, and therefore I have not forgotten briefly to make you a partaker thereof . . . to the right reverend godly learned father, my very good friend, Mr. John Foxe, preacher of the Word of God.

He was moreover a notable preacher, and one of his sermons, which resulted from his converting a Spanish Jew, was so famous that Sir Francis Walsingham, then in bed, sent to him and ordered a repeat and private performance in his bedroom.

But most important of all, for it goes to the heart of his greatest achievement, was his hatred of cruelty and his humanity. We are often told that there was little toleration in the 16th century among Protestants and Catholics, that there was indeed little humanitarian feeling in our modern sense at all, and that we must not look for it and therefore must be kind towards the apparent cruelty of the persecutions. And that is as true as most historical generalizations. But it is not the whole truth, and of all Englishmen it is the author of the *Acts and Monuments* who is the shining exception.

Few Christians in that age had any thought of toleration for those who denied the Divinity of Christ, or the Holy Trinity: such denials seemed to them not so much heresy as open blasphemy. But when Joan of Kent was burned in 1550 on the condemnation of Cranmer, Foxe went to John Rogers and begged him to intercede for the woman, "that at least the life of the wretched woman might be spared"— and when Rogers replied that the death penalty must be inflicted Foxe said what was that but to borrow from the "papal laws and bring into the Christian arena the torments of this dreadful death", whereat, fatefully, on Rogers still disagreeing Foxe

> held his friend's right hand in a firm grasp and beating it with his own right hand said, "Well, maybe the day will come when you yourself will have your hands full of this same gentle burning."

In the reign of Elizabeth a congregation of Anabaptists was discovered in London in 1575; twenty-seven were seized and five were imprisoned and menaced with the fire. It was then Foxe wrote to the Queen a letter which deserves inclusion in any anthology of great Christian letters:

> I defend them not: these errors should be repressed, and I rejoice that no Englishman is infected therewith . . . [it is the manner of their punishment which shocks me . . .] to burn up with fiery flame, blazing with pitch and sulphur the living bodies of wretched men who err through blindness of judgment is a hard thing and belongs more to the spirit of Rome than to the spirit of the Gospel . . . nor do I favour the lives of men alone: would that I could succour the very beasts too. For such is my disposition (I will say this of myself, foolishly perhaps, but yet truly) that I can scarce pass the shambles where beasts are slaughtered, but that my mind secretly recoils with a feeling of pain . . . the one thing I earnestly beg that you suffer not the pyres and flames of Smithfield, so long laid to sleep under your blessed auspices, to rekindle now.

At a time when his own name stood on a black list at Rome of those marked out for execution should the opportunity arise, Foxe (and this was strange indeed for a 16th-century Protestant) interceded for the Jesuit Campion, pleading that the sentence be commuted to some less dreadful end.

He was, as I say, prematurely aged, worn out by his own austerities, one of those restless spirits born to burn themselves out, and incapable of slowing up; an odd character, a little perhaps of a crank, and yet beloved as "Father Foxe" to a great multitude of all classes and conditions, to the London poor and to the great Queen herself. So that when he knew his end was near he contrived to send his sons away on urgent business that they might be spared the pain of witnessing his passing. As today you look away from Moorgate Street across the bleak waste caused by the blitz there stands erect a burned-out shell of a noble temple, St. Giles Cripplegate, and there, rather appropriately, John Foxe lies buried.

Foxe began to write about the persecutions of Christians as early as 1552 and may have been put on the theme by the Lady Jane Grey herself. This was long before the shadow of things to come had fallen across the English path, and he intended a history of the persecutions in Europe with special reference to the Wycliffites and Lollards, about whom little was known on the Continent. Latin was his best language for writing, and he wrote in Latin with an eye to Continental readers. He had a great part of the book ready when he went into exile and the book was dedicated on August 31, 1554, to Duke Christopher of Württemberg. It is a small book of 212 pages and begins with the words "Commentarii rerum in ecclesia gestarum . . ."

Then, in 1555, the burnings began. John Rogers, as John Bradford wrote, "valiantly broke the ice", and thereafter the spate of victims continued. There were about three hundred in all, and the burnings did not begin until half way through the reign. They began with the most eminent and famous, in the hope that lesser folk would profit from this dire example. Then, apart from a lull in the middle, they went on, on an average one or two a week to the end of the reign. Once the old laws for dealing with heretical pravity had been revived there was plenty of scope for a reign of terror. But the procedure was a curious mixture of old and new, of royal initiative, of commission and proclamation, and since there were no longer religious orders to take an initiative in the detection of heresy a new power was given to the secular arm, and mayors and justices of the peace were told off to present suspected heresies at the regular sessions of Oyer and Terminer. Who was responsible really for the persecution? Not, I think, the bishops. There is more than one sign that it troubled Gardiner, and his proud choleric nature had unexpected moments of gentleness and once there escaped from him, when upbraided for cruelty, a revealing denial—"some there be that think this be the best way". Nor, I think, Bonner, though the story of his bloody mindedness is much more than a legend invented by Foxe. When Queen Elizabeth came to her throne she made two public gestures to delight the people: she kissed the Bible and she refused to let Bonner kiss her hand. But still there were indignant letters from the Council to Bonner complaining of his slowness and lethargy and reluctance to put the savage laws in execution. We must look higher up, and while modern historians are inclined, on rather slender grounds, to excuse King Philip of Spain, there is something to be said for the hint given in Foxe's appeal to the nobility of England in 1557:

> Does the queen need spurring on to this work? Nay, she is a very fury for the slaughter. Restrain the theologians, I beg of you.

I am afraid some of the responsibility rests there: on the doctrinaire bigotry of theological divines who had been the bane of the later Middle Ages and were as cordially hated by More and Erasmus as by the reformers. And on the sad, pathetic figure of a princess whose faith and devotion ran through the sour channels of embittered memories of wasted tragic years: it was as if every moment of the sins that made the Reformation through the betrayal of Katherine of Arragon were revisited on the children of those who made the Reformation.

Early in 1555 precious, first-hand documents began to

reach Foxe, the last notebook of John Rogers fished out of his prison cell by his son Daniel under the very noses of the guards: letters of Hooper in prison, copies of the great disputations at Oxford of Latimer, Cranmer and Ridley. But soon the news could not keep pace. In 1556 two Reformers wrote to Bullinger:

> so great is the number of martyrs . . . that those godly men who on a former occasion made it their business to enquire into this matter, are now unable to ascertain either the number or the names of the sufferers.

As Mr. Mozley says, "If it had been hard to trace the story of the divines who suffered in 1555, it was hopeless to expect to do so with the obscure and humble victims of the last years of the reign."

It has often been said that these humbler people were anabaptists and radicals who would have been burned under Henry VIII, Edward VI, or Elizabeth, anyway. And it has been suggested that Foxe suppressed the details about them because they were radicals. But that is not so. In the first place he does not flinch throughout his work to give the details of the more extreme sectaries who suffered, and in the second, he himself was the one person who had pleaded for the lives of such radicals. Most of the indictments touched two questions in the reign of Mary, the Papal authority and the Sacrament of the Altar, and I suspect that the latter was the leading question for which most of them were burned.

Though we must not play down the importance of the eminent martyrs, it is important to note that the majority came from the lower orders of society. Of the gentry, 166 went safely into exile and but nine came to the fire. So that there is truth in Thomas Fuller's words:

> Always in time of persecution, the church is like a copse which hath in it more under wood than oaks. For great men consult with their safety, while the poorer sort boldly embrace religion with both arms.

E

The Marian martyrs included "thirteen weavers, four fullers, two tailors, seven husbandmen, six labourers, three brewers, two butchers, one miller, two bricklayers, two carpenters, three sawyers, three painters, one glazier".

We may notice here one evidence of the infiltration of the English Bible. The Catholic historian Philip Hughes says of the martyrs:

> Through their habitual frequenting of the Bible, these people have, for themselves, become transformed into scriptural figures, and all the drama of their lives, has itself become transformed into a scriptural event, itself a part of and a continuation of the sacred story.

But not only to themselves did this appear so: that Bottom the Weaver and Snout the Tinker found that, like Feeble the Tailor, they "owed God a Death" is testimony to the fact that the groundlings were now the actors in an epic, and it is a portent in religious history that new layers of social environment had become articulate and competent in what Fuller calls "their real sermon of patience at their death".

The first edition of Foxe's famous *Book of Martyrs* was written in Latin and appeared in Basle in 1559 from the press of Oporinus. The title reads: "A commentary of the events that happened in the Church in these last perilous times, and mostly of the great persecutions throughout Europe, and of God's holy martyrs, and other notable things, arranged by kingdoms and nations . . . Part one, containing the narration of the events in England and Scotland, and particularly of the dread persecution under Mary, lately Queen".

Seldom had a book been more opportune than this, written with almost incredible speed under the shadow of great events, rather as though Churchill's great six volumes had appeared within a few months of the war. The best thing that can be said for the authors of the Marian persecution that it was intended as a gigantic and horrifying propaganda campaign to make men fear. Instead, because of Foxe, it became in reverse the greatest single act of propaganda in history: and much more than that, for we all detest propaganda and in the end it evokes sales-resistance in our minds, but this struck deep into the memory of England, so that the memorial of grave events became itself an historical event counting more than many battles in our national story.

The 1559 volume is a folio of 750 pages divided into six books, reprinting his earlier commentary, while the last four books treat the Marian persecutions, though it is a comment on the character of the documents which had reached him that of 518 pages devoted to the reign of Mary, 338, two-thirds of the book dealt with Hooper, Bradford, Philpot, Latimer, Ridley and Cranmer. This book was indeed intended for foreigners, but when he returned to England he realized his work was but begun: testimonies—first-hand testimonies from the eye witnesses like Dame Honeywood, who lost her shoes in the press of the crowd when she went to see John Bradford burned, and had to hobble home on bare feet: from friends and relatives; and the records of the cut and thrust of deadly disputation or the poignant letters of the martyrs themselves. The result is that in making the next English version he has to abridge, and there are some documents in the first Latin edition which never reappeared, so that the historian cannot neglect any one early edition of the work.

Then the great book appeared *The Acts and Monuments of these last and perilous days*, printed by the printer, friend and landlord of John Foxe, the great John Daye, and appearing March 20, 1563. This is a great folio volume of 1,800 pages. It has a calendar of martyrs arranged according to months and days, and as it has Red and Black letter days and includes Ridley along with St. Michael and All Angels in Red, there was some colour for horrified Catholic protestation. And the work had pictures, sixty of them woodcuts of great power, and such that when one

showed Bonner the picture of himself scourging prisoners
he is said to have cried, "A vengeance on the fool. How did
he get my picture drawn so right?" These simple, vivid
first-hand narratives and the pictures with them had an
absorbing effect on a generation which can only be com-
pared with the modern horrors of the strip cartoon and
television.

It was a huge book and it was dear. But it was a sensation,
and the haste with which Catholics began to answer it with
invective and argument is the best testimony to its effect.
Nicholas Harpsfield wrote *Six Dialogues* in 1566 which
had Foxe as a main target. Thomas Harding in his fight
against Jewell turned aside to assault the *Acts and Monuments* as the "huge dunghill of your stinking martyrs" and
its 1000 lies: the Jesuit Parsons (1603-4) wrote his *Treatise
of the Three Conversions of England* mainly against Foxe. Yet
even these could not forbear their testimony to its impact.
Harpsfield has to confess that he has "searched out . . .
matters accurately and laboriously". Parsons says that the
book

> hath done more hurt alone to simple souls in our country
> by infecting and poisoning them unawares under the bait
> of pleasant histories, fair pictures, and painted pageants,
> than the other most pestilent books together.

What to us seems the crude side of the book probably was
not the least esteemed by the original readers: the marginal
notes, "Here is Bonner in a Pelting chafe", "Mark a whole-
some company of caterpillars", are often rather naïve, and
the No Popery is of a more stubborn fighting common-
sense kind, than the reasoned apologetic of Cranmer, Jewell
or Hooker.

Meanwhile Foxe got on with a new edition, for documents of all kinds came pouring in, and he and his friends
began to search the bishops' registers in England and Scotland. A great deal had to be cut. A new motif in the work
is to show that the Protestants are the true, old Church and

have their pedigree which stretches back to apostolic times. And he increases the woodcuts from 60 to 150, so that the new edition of 1570 is of two great folio volumes with 2,300 pages of text, divided into double columns. This great volume is, as Mozley says, "the crown of his career", the fruit of long and wearisome, gigantic labours of mind and spirit. Like the previous editions, the work has new and notable prefaces, to the Queen, and a moving appeal for Christian unity to the English nation. There followed a third edition in 1576, almost a reprint of the second, but of inferior paper and print. The fourth edition of 1584 has larger pages, and is greatly improved, and contains 2,154 pages in two volumes. This was the last in his life-time, though the posthumous edition of 1596 may contain some of his handiwork. The eight-volume 19th-century editions suffered greatly from being not very well edited, but they are still indispensable for the historian of the period and a mine of important first-hand documents, more fascinating than any textbooks or secondary studies, even though the one-volume edition has, as devotional reading, survived only among the more extreme Protestant wings of the English churches.

Foxe is not a scientific historian: but his blemishes are those of contemporary humanism, and as a scholar he can more than stand the comparison with Martin Bucer or even the great Erasmus. He worked in huge haste and was sometimes careless: he makes slips of detail which are not always ironed out later. He is at the mercy of his information and some of those who transcribed records for him were less careful than he was. Sometimes, where a writer like John Rogers, in the notes of the final speech which he was not allowed to give, writes "etc. etc." Foxe will fill out the etcetera and say what he thinks Rogers would have said. Sometimes he describes (but not often) a martyr who was soon shown to be very much alive by the screams of Foxe's opponents. Almost all his geese are swans: and his swans often turn out to be very queer and ugly ducklings.

But swans there were—John Frith and William Tyndale, John Rogers and John Bradford, Hugh Latimer and Nicholas Ridley, Thomas Cranmer—men of whom any section of the church catholic and any Christian nation might be proud; and when we think of them, John Frith 25, William Tyndale 41, Nicholas Ridley in the prime of life, we think of the glories of the English Church which they might have shaped had they not been turned to dust and ashes.

Foxe felt the cruelty of it: he was honest and indignant and passionate enough to put his passion into words, never sublime or very moving words, but plain straightforward writing—indeed the vast work as a whole reads like a repetitive monotonous sermon with but two points and those driven home endlessly: the cruelty of popery, the witness of the martyrs.

Few English Protestants would speak of the Church of Rome today as did their 16th-century forbears. But we may remember that the cry of "No Popery" was a centuries old complaint, not against the modern papacy, but the unreformed mediaeval Church, with its enormous legal and financial Circumlocution Office, its inefficiency, chicanery and shoddiness, its entanglement of laws and jurisdictions, its obsession with the great games of diplomacy and power politics; and all of this, more criminally, bringing the souls of men into bondage to the very kind of religion of law from which Christ came to set men free. The Inquisition in Spain, the persecutions in France and in the Netherlands, these seemed terribly of a piece with the concentrated fury of the Marian fires. I think I can understand good Christian men coming to believe that this realm of England must strike free and clean, and the growing determination of millions of Englishmen to have it no more. Anyway, there it was, stubborn, honest—if you like, obtuse: but it gave a turn and a temper to the new religious way of life of Englishmen which has not yet been entirely eradicated.

Professor Haller and his pupils have shown how Foxe's view of history influenced the apocalyptic nationalism of Puritan England. What they have not noticed is that Foxe in setting his chronicles within a wider view of the whole sweep of Christian history has borrowed from the great German "Magdeburg Centuries" of Flaccius Illyricus, the view of history in terms of the rise and overthrow of Anti-Christ, but giving it an English dress.

Now, if it is bad form nowadays to write about Popery, how much more Non-U is it to speak of the Papacy as Anti-Christ. And yet S. T. Coleridge wrote wisely when he said:

> If by Anti-Christ is meant . . . a power in the Christian church which in the name of Christ, and at once pretending and usurping his authority, is systematically subversive of the essential and distinguishing characters and purposes of the Christian church: that then, if the papacy be not Anti-Christ the guilt of schism in its most aggravated form, lies on the authors of the Reformation. For nothing less than this could have justified so tremendous a rent in the Catholic church, with all its foreseen most calamitous consequences. And so Luther thought and so thought Wycliffe before him.
>
> *(On the Church and State)*

The Magdeburg Centuries, and Foxe, after them, thus set their chronicles within a dynamic interpretation of Christian history, but not pessimistically conceived, not capitulating to the extravagancies of mediaeval and Protestant sectaries, who had similarly evaluated history in terms of the five kingdoms in the Book of Daniel. For it evokes the militant character of the Church, puts the martyrs in their real perspective and significance, as testifying beyond themselves to the power of evil in this present age, and beyond this, yet more decisively to the victory of Christ, the conqueror of death and hell.

To turn from Foxe's *Book of Martyrs* to such a modern

volume as the anthology, edited by Helmuth Gollwitzer,[1] of those who died for their convictions under the Nazi régime is to move within the same world of crisis, conviction, and courage at the last. Here, in Foxe, is Anne Askew, tortured on the rack in the Tower, manhandled by the Lord Chancellor himself, to make her confess the names of her friends, in an attempt to implicate ladies of the Court, and if possible the Queen Katherine Parr herself: so that her swollen body must be carried off in a chair to Smithfield at her execution. But she did not yield. In the modern anthology is the young French school teacher Anne Marie Colin, captured when trying to smuggle her children across the border, who wrote a poem on the eve of her execution,

> I will betray tomorrow,
> But not today.

You may put beside it the verse which John Hooper wrote with coal on the window of the New Inn, Gloucester, before his burning:

> Of earthly tyrant, have thou no dread.
> God's Word, which is thy compass,
>   shall thee guide
> And the wind is fair.

The final contribution, therefore, of Foxe's book is not sectarian nor partisan. To an age which roughly and too hastily, perhaps, had rejected the massive solidarity of mediaeval commerce with heaven, with the church triumphant, Foxe's book restored the dimensions of eternity, the eschatological horizon of decision, the life-and-death character of the Christian vocation. If Francis Drake read it aloud to his little company at sea as they nosed into unknown seas, on a desperate adventure: if Nicholas Gidding read it regularly to his quieter company in hardly more explored realms of the human spirit: if John Wesley chose it first of all the Christian classics, to be woven into that

[1] *Dying We Live* (Eng. tr., 1956).

Christian library which he prepared for the edification of his preachers, it was because it spoke beyond the limitations of any century or land, of "the noble army of martyrs", and the continuing, blessed warfare of the Church militant here on earth, and of the greatest of all solidarities, our companionship in that City of God which "is seated partly in the course of these declining times, but chiefly in that solid estate of eternity".

CHAPTER IV

JOHN MILTON
AND "PARADISE LOST"

THE great movement known as Puritanism profoundly
affected the whole temper of the English and American
peoples. In the last few years an impressive series of learned
studies has put Puritanism in better perspective and in a
more favourable light: much in the traditional view of
Puritanism springs from hostile prejudice, while even
Macaulay's Puritan turns out, often, to be a Clapham
evangelical in fancy dress. "If we take Puritan culture as a
whole", said Professor Perry Miller, "we shall find that
about 90 per cent. of the intellectual life, scientific knowledge, morality, manners and customs, notions and prejudices, was that of all Englishmen. The other 10 per cent.
made all the difference."

In its widest sense Puritanism echoed something in the
changing mood of the late 16th century, its austerity and
introspection, mirrored for us in *Hamlet*, in Rembrandt's
self-portraits, or the poems of Donne, and reflected in
that characteristic Puritan literature, the spiritual autobiography, the diary. It is a concern with conscience, and
with those intimations of mortality to be found in the
writings of Sir Walter Raleigh as truly as in the sermons of
Richard Baxter a generation later. It was no doubt, to use
Toynbee's metaphor, a "response" to the "challenge" of the
humanism of the Elizabethan age. It has often been pointed
out that the literature of the Puritans, with the recurring
themes of spiritual warfare, has family resemblance to the
old Desert Fathers, and Bunyan's story of the fight with
Apollyon recaptures the strenuous fervour of the classic

74

temptations of St. Anthony of Egypt. Seventeenth century austerity, like 17th-century scholasticism, was in part a genuine continuity with the Middle Ages, and it links Jesuits, Laudians and Puritans together. But essentially Puritanism was a ferment within the Protestant movement —in Milton's words, a movement "for the reform of reformation". The Church of England had kept its continuity with the mediaeval church by retaining the historic episcopate and the historic succession: it had done so, its critics thought, by retaining other things less happy—abuses of practice, and perversions of pastoral care which on the Continent had been purged out by the Council of Trent, or dealt with in the legislation of the Reformed and Lutheran churches. From the very beginning of the English Reformation there had been a dissident ferment which as time went on became more and more influential. One great matter focused attention, that great third dimension of Protestant Churchmanship which added to the theme "Word and Sacrament" that of the "discipline of Christ", a phrase which in the 17th century covered the vexed problem of the polity of the church itself.

This was the problem. It sounds rather simple. It was— we use the word advisedly—devilishly complex. The question whether the godly magistrate has the right of reforming the church, answered differently by Luther, Zwingli, Oecolampadius and the Anabaptists, prepared for generations of Protestant controversy on the Continent and in England. But in England there came in the latter part of the 16th century, with a new generation, a truculent Presbyterianism and a rigid Anglicanism battling for control of the English church. Outside these were a growing number of Separatists who could not accept the mixed communities of a State Church and who formed their own "gathered church" either on the basis of a voluntary covenant or of the sacrament of Baptism, and who kept firm hold on their own prerogative of discipline. As the 17th century proceeded, and in the toleration made inevitable by civil war, more and more radical groups of Puritans emerged—the Quakers, the Levellers, Diggers, and the Fifth Monarchy men. And there were those, sometimes called "Seekers", who passed restlessly from one group to another, at odds with all institutional religion.

Modern studies have brought out the importance of Puritanism as a religious and theological movement, and drawn attention to the Cambridge Puritans, that movement of dons and younger scholars which produced a great succession of learned divines, from St. John's and Christ's colleges especially, and from the newer foundations of Emmanuel and Sidney Sussex colleges. They made a deep impact on two generations, and if the reaction and in some ways the antithesis of their Calvinist scholasticism came in the Cambridge Platonists, it was in those same colleges and from their pupils. Many of these men were Anglicans and Puritans: learned divines, like the great William Perkins and William Ames, who were renowned across Europe and deeply influential in America; great preachers like the famous Laurence Chaderton, to whom the crowded audience in Great St. Mary's cried out at the close of two hours, "For God's sake, sir, go on! go on!", and John Preston who, though he hobnobbed with politicians and dangerously won the favour of the King, refused to abandon his good craft of preaching. Many of them were devoted pastors, giving themselves in little villages, like Richard Greenham and the famous "Decalogue" Dodd, labouring to be understood of simple folk. "Poor simple people," they said of Dodd, "that never knew what religion meant, when they had gone to hear him, could not choose but talk of his sermon. It mightily affected poor creatures to hear the mysteries of God . . . brought down to their own language and dialect." In his own home Dodd kept Liberty Hall, for he was famous for good conversation, and talked all through dinner, and "when he was faint, would call for a small glass of beer, and wine mixed, and then to it again until midnight". They passed on their love of learning to the New World. "In contrast to all other pioneers", says Perry Miller of the American Puritan, "they made no concession to the forest, but in the midst of frontier conditions, in the very throes of clearing the land and erecting shelters, they maintained schools and a college, a standard of scholarship and of competent writing, a class of men devoted entirely to the life of the mind and of the soul."

We speak today, then, of Puritan humanism, in a way which 19th-century historians hardly spoke. In the midst of this religious ferment there was an intelligentsia (a stabilizing element which Victorian Nonconformity, excluded from the universities, could not fully supply). It was, to be sure, a narrowed humanism, too confined within the twin Biblical and classical traditions, though it did play some part in the new opening scientific horizons, and the heirs of the Puritans in the Dissenting academies were often forward-looking at a time when the older universities looked back to the older rhetorical traditions in education.

John Milton is the fine flower of Puritan humanism, and in his mind was blended a great storehouse of classical and Hebraic culture. He was born, appropriately, under the sign of the "Spread Eagle" in Bread Street, Cheapside, on Friday, December 9, 1608, the son of a scrivener who, besides bestowing on his son a love of music, dedicated him as a child "to the pursuits of literature". He gave him learned tutors before sending him at the age of 12 to St. Paul's school, and at the age of 17 to Cambridge. There "our lady of Christ's" was often driven to assert a toughness which belied his long hair and pale countenance, as well as to an open attack on the backward-looking rhetorical tradition of contemporary university learning. He soon gave promise as a poet, and his lovely ode "On the Morning of Christ's Nativity", at the age of 21, has something of that blend of classical and scriptural which we find in Michelangelo's ceiling in the Sistine chapel, where the Sibyls and the Prophets gesticulate side by side. In an earlier age he would undoubtedly have sought a career in the Church, but he grew up amid a mounting tension against the Establishment and against the clergy and he refused to "subscribe slave", regarding himself as "church outed" by the prelates, and turned his thoughts to a prophetic vocation not as a priest, nor yet as a divine, but to the vocation of a poet.

He made the Grand Tour, and this became for him in Italy itself, uncompromising and vociferous Protestant that he was, a triumph and a progress, while his skill in Latin and in Italian roused scholars and ecclesiastics to courteous admiration. Across these learned delights, and the promise of his ripening powers, there fell the dark shadow of the church struggle and of civil strife. As into the solemn calm of *Lycidas* there comes the rough, angry complaint of Christians for the hungry sheep unfed, so now he interrupted his own dreams and returned manfully, with the responsibility which in modern times was saluted in the return to Germany from America in 1939 of a Dietrich Bonnhoeffer (for our concern in this chapter is less with Milton as a poet than as a Christian man).

In the Civil War itself he played a vigorous part, first as a pamphleteer. No Christian writer, unless it be Luther, since the beginning of the Reformation had such an immense power of invective; he could and he did fulfil what Mr. C. S. Lewis calls the mark of the great polemical writer, of rebuking magnificently. In his pamphlets he combines a classical vocabulary with an immense power over words of Anglo-Saxon derivation, so that he employs all manner of dialectical armoury, the verbal equivalent of pike and musket, of cavalry charge and artillery, and then, at the end of some devastating sentence, he will throw away all weapons and seize his opponent's throat or punch him on the nose. The immense power of this invective seems to have been lost on his contemporaries: his pamphlets were not best sellers. The simple forthrightness of the pamphlets of Walwyn or Lilburne went down much better with the man in the street or the trooper in the army. But into Milton's prose there comes not only a savage, humourless, arrogant anti-clericalism; not only an intransigent, fierce, unyielding Protestantism; but the new hopeful, apocalyptic vision of what God may be planning to do on the earth, the wonderful new things he wills to reveal through his Englishmen, and the magnificent conviction that to be the poet laureate of this new order might be his own vocation—his own conviction that he had it in him to pen something which men would not willingly let die.

In this chapter we have chosen to be concerned with his great epic, *Paradise Lost*. We have included this in the company of great religious "bestsellers" which have been acclaimed by the testimony of Christian common sense. And yet it may well be that he deserves his place alongside the makers of the English Bible and the Prayer Book, not for his best seller but for his worst seller.

We cannot speak of what he has written for Christian men without some tribute to his exposition of the case for Christian toleration, and his view of Christian truth, immortally enshrined in that pamphlet, *Areopagitica*, which was as far ahead of his own age, and perhaps of himself, as it is of our own century. Although Milton's works seem almost classically free from the subjectivisim of so many Puritan writers, there were two points in his own private life, where what Luther called *Anfechtung* struck deeply home, and were reflected in his writing. The one was his blindness, the other his unhappy first marriage. His pathetic marriage and separation from Mary Powell, in some ways parallel with the tragedy of another knight of English prose, John Ruskin, brought for him an immense personal crisis, and one by-product of it was the radical view of divorce which he obtruded into public notice in 1644, when there were enough grave matters of contention before a Presbyterian Government, than this matter for which Milton could find no better authority in tradition than a long-neglected tract of Martin Bucer (who also had a concern about divorce). So that Milton's attack on the

Presbyterian censorship of books was a by-product of a by-product, which must have seemed very much a diversion from the main object of his dedicated writing. Yet in it his prose style is tamed of an exuberance which sometimes verges on eccentricity, and becomes quietly eloquent and majestic. For this pamphlet calls attention to the greatest of all the moral victories of the Puritan period. Professor Jordan has said that it saw one of the most momentous changes in the history of English thought, the growth of a rationale, which included a Christian rationale, of toleration. When the shouting and tumult of Naseby and Dunbar had died away, those *Magnalia Dei per Anglos suos*, and when Captain Cromwell and King Charles were in the dust, it was possible to realize that rack and thumbscrew, knife and branding iron, bullet and cavalry charge and push of pike, and execution block, can dispose very successfully of bodies but cannot kill a single idea. That truth is diverse and many-sided, that catholicity demands not uniformity but variety, that unity and uniformity are not the same—the ideas which are the marrow of modern ecumenicity—would have seemed to most 16th- and 17th-century Christians like the apostolic nightmare in which St. Peter beheld a sheet full of all manner of creeping things. The intellectual ferment which produced 22,000 pamphlets between 1640 and 1660 seemed to most leaders of Church and State, Anglican and Puritan, a very horrid thing. Only a Milton could see it instead as something wonderful.

The shop of war hath not more anvils and hammers working to fashion out plates and instruments of armed justice, in defence of beleaguered truth, than there be pens and heads there, sitting by their studious lamps, musing and searching, revolving new notions and ideas to present the approaching reformation.

That was why he saw England as mighty and puissant as an eagle,

while the whole noise of timorous and flocking birds
with those also who love the twilight, flutter about,
amazed at what she means, and in their envious gabble
would prognosticate a year of sects and schisms.

It is true that in fact toleration was established by the
tired politicians and not by prophetic voices. But it counts
that in this period there was a Christian rationale of toleration, such as had already been voiced by Thomas Helwys
and by Roger Williams, but now found a classical habitation
and enduring name.

But Milton does more than attack with biting satire a
womanish fear of truth which has found new Puritan expression in a censorship as bad as anything in Rome. He
goes to the heart of the failure of all legalism, the weakness
of Puritanism that it is always trying to force the moral
pace, and to impose by law, or the sanctions of moral
influence, outward forms of a godliness which could only
come from within, a legalism which must in the end turn
Puritanism itself into a petrified and unlovely thing.

If we think to regulate printing, thereby to rectify
manners, we must regulate all recreations and pastimes
all that is delightful to man. No music must be heard, no
song be set or sung but what is grave or doric . . . who
shall forbid and separate all idle resort, all evil company?

And so he speaks, and the words count for our good
doctrinaire modern Puritans:

These things will be, and must be: but how they shall
be least hurtful, how least enticing, herein consists
the grave and governing wisdom of a State. To sequester
out of the world into Atlantic and utopian politics which
can never be drawn into use, will not mend our condition:
but to ordain wisely as in this world of evil, in the midst
whereof God hath placed us unavoidably.

The argument has two great main thrusts. The first is
F

the assertion that the search for truth is an occupation for which men and women must at all costs be free. He speaks back to those in the 16th century who feared the "open Bible", and he speaks forward to those who in our time would still revive intellectual witch hunting, in the most famous of all his sentences:

> I cannot praise a fugitive and cloistered virtue un-exercised and unbreathed, that never sallies out and seeks her adversary but slinks out of the race where that immortal garland is to be run for, not without dust and heat.

The other major point is the magnificent description of the unity of truth which "indeed came once into the world with her divine master and was a perfect shape most glorious to look upon". But that unity has been long destroyed and the "sad friends of truth" are still seeking for what have been lost and divided. "We have not found them yet, lords and commons, nor ever shall do till her Master's second coming."

The great argument comes to its noble climax in the next paragraph:

> They are the troublers, they are the dividers of unity who neglect and permit not others to unite those dis-severed pieces which are yet wanting to the body of truth. To be still searching what we know not, by what we know, still closing up truth to truth as we find it (for all her body is homogeneal and proportional), this is the golden rule in theology as well as in arithmetic and makes up the best harmony in a church: not the forced and out-ward union of cold, and neutral and inwardly divided minds.

And if one should object that Milton's thought here is Greek rather than Biblical, one would none the less have to ask whether what he says is true, and whether if it be true it is not testimony to the ultimate wholeness of truth in the Lord of the Scriptures and of all creation who came once on earth, and shall come again.

Despite Milton's close association with the Cromwellian government, as Latin Secretary, and as the literary defender of the regicides, and as the author of a great apologia for the Puritan revolution addressed to the attention of Europe, there was for him a growing disillusion and a fading of the brave vision so nobly expounded in 1644. He had a narrow escape at the Restoration, and was allowed to retire. The eagle had grown to full stature, had spread his wings, but now was a blinded eagle. What blindness means to any man in the shape of *Anfechtung*, the kind of spiritual testing which shakes a life to its foundations, since it calls in question the integrity of God's ways with us, can only be imagined. What it meant to a great poet whose eyes must always be precious gates to images, when the magic casements were shut for ever, is something even more remote from common understanding. That there was strain, some bitterness, and that old Milton could be a petulant trial to those about him, seems certain. Yet he won through to an acceptance of Providence which was his own personal, individual, spiritual victory, however much it be clothed in Puritan terms.

> Doth God exact day labour, light
>   denied?
> I fondly ask, but Patience to prevent that
>   murmur soon replies . . .
> They also serve, who only stand and wait.

Not that the agony was less, for he himself was to put with exquisite poignancy what blindness means to a poet, a poet whose office Milton viewed as that, above all, of a "seer"—in the sublime apostrophe of Light in the opening of Book III of *Paradise Lost*—

> thou
> Revisit'st not these eyes, that roll in vain

To find thy piercing ray, and find no dawn;
So thick a drop serene hath quenchd their orbs,
Or dim suffusion veil'd.

For many years he had meditated a great work, an epic poem, perhaps using the great Arthurian legends. But he turned in the end to the grand Christian "party line". His blindness had led him to reckon with God's providence concerning himself, to justify the ways of God to John Milton. Now he attempts the great argument, to

assert Eternal Providence and justify the ways
of God to men,

by treating the whole divine Plan of Salvation, the grand theme of the Fall and of original sin, which so obsessed 17th-century Protestantism.

There have been so many studies by great authorities of *Paradise Lost* that we shall do no more than remind the Christian reader to go to the poem itself, to read it and re-read it, having first carefully read through the opening chapters of the Book of Genesis.

In *Paradise Lost* the Genesis story is set, as Christian tradition from the time of the Fathers had already set it, within the cosmic setting of a pre-mundane Fall of the rebel angels. Indeed one of the effects of Milton's poem must have been to stamp this particular profound mythology deep upon the mind of English Christians, who to this day would be hard driven to disentangle the Biblical and traditional aspects of a Christian "party line" which in modern times has been hard pressed, and which needs a good deal of "de-mythologizing". Although Macaulay sharply criticized John Martin's illustrations in the early 19th century, as well depicting the vastness of the Miltonic scenery but reducing the actors to insignificance, Martin's immense caverns and stupendous heights do justice to a real element in the poem. Milton does indeed, by indirect hints rather than by precision, give us a sense of huge distances and great immensities. Like modern science fiction, he takes us out into space, so that we come to the tragic incident in the garden of Eden as to a strange planet, to that last star which the astronomers have never seen, our own earth,

> hanging in a golden chain,
> This pendant world, in bigness as a star,
> Of smallest magnitude close by the moon.

Yet, as Sir Walter Raleigh pointed out, this solitary happening on a tiny outpost of the vast universe is of pivotal significance in the great purpose of the ages,

the scene of the action is universal space. The time represented is eternity. The characters are God and his creatures. And all these are exhibited in the clearest and most inevitable relation with the main event, so that there is not an incident, hardly a line of the poem, but leads backwards or forwards to those central lines in the Ninth book:

> So saying, her rash hand in evil hour,
> Forth reaching to the fruit, she plucked, she
> ate.
> Earth felt the wound and Nature from her
> seat
> Sighing through all her works, gave signs of
> woe
> That all was lost.

But this human fall is discovered to us in the context of the angelic rebellion, the superhuman disaster of the fall of the rebel angels. Milton begins with the modern technique of the "flash back", with the moment when the jarring thud of the immense fall of Satan through space has just ceased to reverberate.

> Him the Almighty power
> Hurl'd headlong flaming from the ethereal
> sky,

With hideous ruin and combustion down
To bottomless perdition: there to dwell in
Adamantine chains and penal fire. . . .
Nine times the space that measures day and night
To mortal men, he with his horrid crew
Lay vanquished, rolling in the fiery gulf
Confounded though immortal.

There follows the immense drama of the diabolic council, the "great consult". Yet what a dramatic problem it is, to make real what must on any showing be hopeless, the continued revolt against complete defeat by an Almighty God. Milton succeeds in giving reality to this hopeless situation. There is on another dimension a faint analogy in the situation at the end of World War II in that fantastic bunker in Berlin, where an already defeated Hitler none the less succeeded in inspiring those around him with his own belief in his own power, talking, moving on a board divisions of troops which had no longer any real existence in the world outside—yet making his own fantasy real, and real to those around him, though the cause was finally lost and irretrievably hopeless.

Much has been written of Milton's Satan and his companions. They are certainly very different from the mediaeval devils, either the clumsy, laughable clodhoppers of the miracle plays, or the savagely cruel tormentors of Dante's vision, or of the paintings of Breughel and of Bosch. They are not "dirty Devils": they do not infect our minds with a sense of evil, unless it be that of pride and implacable malice. What Karl Barth says about the Devil, that we had better ignore him, since that is most hateful to him, and that he must have in his nature the weakness of his sin, seems far away from Satan here, this defeated field marshal who might, one feels, come out rather well from a War Crimes Trial.

Milton's characters are intended to be superhuman, but they tend to be inhuman. Adam and Eve again, are not the familiar figures of the more homely mediaeval world's imaging: Adam is a regal, patriarchal figure, a public person of great dignity—not at all the cowering apotheosis of the "little man" who lurks behind Father Abraham in the "Limbo Patrum", the supreme bungler of history, the mediaeval Charlie Chaplin. Here is one who can talk with high Archangels with his own proper sense of dignity. And Eve, the archetype of all "foolish women". We think of that sublime portal of the great Munster of Strasbourg: there on one side the wise virgins: on the other the foolish ones, the most foolish of all who is smiling, casting to the ground her vessel of oil, who in her folly has no knowledge at all of what she is missing. By her side is Eve, Type of all "foolish women"—and on the back of Eve there is a toad and a serpent (the very two forms which Satan assumes in Milton's poem). But Milton's Eve is a "grande dame" indeed, the mother of all dragons, all universal Dames, the First Suffragette.

Milton carefully shows us the responsibility of Man by giving our parents due warning from the Archangel, and by asserting the freedom of Adam.

> God made thee perfect, not immutable;
> And good he made thee: but to persevere
> He left it in thy power: ordain'd thy will
> By nature free, not over-ruled by fate
> Inextricable or strict necessity:
> Our voluntary service he requires,
> Not our necessitated.

There is moreover an ominous, though innocent, pre-echo of the approaching tragedy in Eve's dream, despite the reassuring

> be not sad.
> Evil into the mind of God or man
> May come and go, so unapproved and leave
> No spot or blame behind.

Book IX is the part of this work which to Christian preachers and teachers will most repay careful study. For if it is the presentation of a myth, there has gone to its making much skill and a good deal of profound observation of the character of temptation, of evil and of the working of the human conscience.

The day begins with a tiny cloud on the horizon, a friendly argument about how the day shall be spent, which results in the fateful separation of Adam and Eve, leaving her alone at the mercy of the tempter. Professor Tillyard, the most scholarly and balanced of all modern commentators on Milton, has shown how Milton's view of the Fall is related to that hierarchical view of the Universe which was the "Elizabethan World-Picture" and indeed the classical Christian tradition for many centuries before. It is the conception of the Universe as a great pyramid of authorities, each rank in the hierarchy of existence being bound by duties and rights to that above and below him. It is beautifully and profoundly expressed in the 16th century in the Book of Homilies, and assumed by Shakespeare in the famous speech:

> Take but degree away, untune that string,
> And hark what discord follows.

Here Adam's place in the Genesis narrative is all-important: God has given him dominion over all creation. Eve is next in command, but no more than a first mate of a ship can take over while the captain is on the bridge may she usurp his authority. To do so is much more than a personal disobedience, it is an affront to the order of the Universe: which is why this one act is able, from such small beginning, to become disaster for the whole human story, like the un-winding of a skein of wool. The rebellion of Eve, by taking the initiative in disobeying God's commands, and the acceptance of her usurpation by Adam, is of the utmost importance in the poem. The heart of the tragedy, the temptation by Satan, the flattery, the act of disobedience, is told perhaps more poignantly and though simply, not less profoundly, in Genesis: but it is Milton who elaborates all the subtle inner consequences, and draws the moral, and shows us fallen man, as by a powerful new definition, an excuse-making animal. Thus, profoundly, the book ends:

> Thus they in mutual accusation spent
> The fruitless hours, but neither self condemning,
> And of their vain contest appear'd no end.

There is a good deal here about the nature of evil: pride we have had dissected for us in an anatomy of Satan. Here we see the weakness of evil, the subtle power of flattery. And then a great truth, just when we are thinking in high-faluting terms of an elaborate analysis, that sinners must be at least interesting material for a psychiatrist's notebook; it seems in the end that the Fall occurred because Eve was just hungry, and it was dinner time,

> the hour of noon drew on, and waked
> An eager appetite, raised by the smell
> So Savoury of that fruit.

What follows takes us through a whole gamut of emotions, from anger and passion, and recrimination, and remorse and guilt and fear, to penitence and to the sad but not hopeless calm with which the poem closes. Now can be stated to sinful men the need to trust in divine Providence.

> Henceforth I learn, that to obey is best,
> And love with fear, the only God: to walk
> As in his Presence, ever to observe
> His providence and on him sole depend.

There are no "mystic joys of penitence": no premonition of glorious hope, but as the departing parents of the race look back towards the Paradise they have lost, we feel with them the pain of leaving a dear abode.

Some natural tears they dropt, but wiped
them soon.
The world was all before them, where to
choose
Their place of rest, and Providence their
guide;
They, hand in hand, with wandering steps
and slow,
Through Eden took their solitary way.

That Milton's belief in the Person of Christ was Arian,
finds support in his doctrinal commonplace book, but is
hardly to be alleged from his poem, for nobody could give
dramatic form to the Plan of Salvation, and to the Incarna-
tion and Redemption of mankind through the Eternal Son,
and present his intervention in history against an eternal
background, without raising intolerable theological tensions,
which the classical theologians evade by not pressing home
their metaphors. More serious is the charge that for him
God is the Great Taskmaster rather than the God and
Father of our Lord Jesus Christ, that the Son of God is a
splendid being, but like Satan, inhuman rather than very
Man. But in all this Milton, if he erred, erred with many
of his generation. It was an unwholesome trend in Puritan
theology at this time that it had overstressed the sovereign
will of God: that it had made too much of his hidden counsels and his secret will. Indeed we may wonder whether in fact
it had not made the Fall, rather than the Cross of Christ,
the pivot of the human story: been preoccupied with the
implications of the doctrine of sin, rather than with the hope
of a regenerated mankind and a re-made universe. Certainly
the 19th- and 20th-century Christians have a task of de-
mythologizing at this point, and of examining, as the great
F. D. Maurice began to do, the possibilities of a Christ-
centred anthropology, a doctrine of man, and of the Fall,
which in the light of Colossians and Ephesians should be
Christ-centred, setting the first Adam within the greater

context of the second Adam, and all within what Charles Wesley calls "His mercy's whole Design". Not all that this great Christian poem said to Christian men in the 17th-century has survival value for our edification. Yet there is much to ponder, much to meditate, much to learn, from a serious and attentive Christian reading of *Paradise Lost*.

CHAPTER V

JOHN BUNYAN
AND "PILGRIM'S PROGRESS"

PURITANISM began as a learned movement, and for most of its course it became more and more a political movement. But there was a great part of Puritanism which was not learned, in the technical and academic sense. Indeed, the process begun at the Reformation, and of which the vernacular Bible had been one among many instruments, whereby other social levels became religiously competent and articulate, was continued. No doubt the whole social escalator was in motion, but the Protestant, Puritan faith gave to little people a dignity and competence in the affairs of the soul. When John Bunyan overheard ordinary housewives in Bedford on their doorsteps discussing Christian experience in the precise terms of Protestant spiritual theology, it was not only a portent in his own inner life, but an emblem of something new in English religion. A few years ago a comic song celebrated the common people of England in terms of "Smith, Jones, Robinson and Brown" —and it is of much significance that in real history, in the 16th and 17th century, there were Puritan leaders Smyth, Johnson, Robinson and Browne. We saw how the trades-men martyrs played their manful part in the church struggle under Mary, preaching not with words but, as Thomas Fuller said, their real sermon of patience. But now the little people began to speak for God. John Bunyan is one of a great number of "mechanick Preachers", along with Benjamin Keach and Vavasour Powell and many others, who gained a good deal of scorn from the well-to-do, but whose simple forthright eloquence, in the simple unembroidered language of the English Bible, eschews the flowery rhetoric of Lancelot Andrewes and Jeremy Taylor, but speaks none the less to the condition of the "gathered Churches" which found during the Commonwealth a liberty of prophesying which was harshly denied them at the Restoration.

Puritanism became a lost cause, and that is one reason—a non-theological factor as we say today—why its vast spiritual and moral theology has vanished. Much of it had no survival value, but there was a good deal more which deserved a better fate, and which preserved a rich tradition of "inward religion" which bore persistent fruit in the devotion of the 18th century. Not for nothing do the Puritans find more attention in the anthology of Wesley's "Christian Library" than any other Christian movement, though Wesley's selections are framed in an almost bewildering Catholicity which includes the Fathers, the Cambridge Platonists and French and Spanish Catholic mystics. Above all there was Puritan moral theology.

It was the age of map-making. The great pioneers had discovered the new world overseas, but at the end of Elizabeth's reign there began the rediscovery of England herself by the antiquarians and the map-makers. In some such way the casuists, Puritan, Anglican, Jesuit, turned to map-making, to charting the country of the soul, the field of moral decision. This practical concern for what modern Americans call "counselling" was bound up with the Puritan concern for pastoral care. In this, as in their scholastic theology and their preaching, there was a genuine continuity with the later Middle Ages. Textbooks were written by the last of the schoolmen, by Gabriel Biel and Chancellor Gerson, on such themes as "Temptations concerning Predestination", long before Calvin. We find the great Puritan casuist William Ames copying down whole sections from the moral theology of William of Paris. But there was a specific Puritan moral theology arising from the doctrinal emphases of Protestantism and its own means of grace, problems concerning election, justification, and our standing with God. Perhaps the most famous of all Puritan titles for such a work is the little tract of William Perkins, *A Case of Conscience: the greatest that ever was: how a man may know whether he be the childe of God: or no.*

The young John Bunyan was not a casuist: he was a case. He suffered from a "bruised conscience". He knew for many years the long spiritual travail for which Luther used the word *Anfechtung.* No wonder that when, during his inner struggles, he found an old English translation of Luther's *Galatians,* so old and tattered that it was almost falling to pieces, he found that it might have been written out of his own heart. That sense of claustrophobia, passing over into agoraphobia in which the guilty soul feels itself forsaken by all, with the whole universe at enmity, face to face with the wrath of God, which Luther describes so often and with a terrible and sombre beauty, has no real compeer in the English language save in Bunyan's own spiritual confession, in his autobiography. And when he speaks of grace and of saving faith, there is no English writer who again and again writes in words which might have been written by Luther himself. "There is nothing like faith at a pinch. Faith dissolves doubts as the sun drives away mists . . . therefore faith must always be in exercise. Faith is the eye, is the mouth, is the hand: and one of these is of use all day long. Faith is to see, to receive, to work, to eat: and a Christian should be seeing or receiving, or working or feeding all day long. Let it rain, let it blow, let it thunder, let it lighten, a Christian must still believe."

That is why a Protestant Christian can understand things about Bunyan that are hidden from the innumerable literary critics who have written some very foolish pages about the measurement of Bunyan's sins, and failed altogether to understand either what it means to have a "bruised conscience" or justification by faith.

John Bunyan was born at Elstow in Bedfordshire, and

it is only a slightly silly modern fashion to assert that he was not a tinker but a brazier. He was surely bred up to be a "mechanick" and knew what it was to tramp the country-side with a pack on his back, and the blessed easement of laying down a burden on the grass. In 1644-7 he seems to have been involved in the Civil War, upon the Parliamentary side. He made a homely marriage, and his wife brought him as her dowry two books, one by a Dissenter, Arthur Dent's *Plain Man's Pathway to Heaven*, and the other Bishop Bayly's *Practice of Piety*—this last a work of edification which ran into many editions and had some real influence in the awakening of German pietism.

The spiritual autobiography, the diary, it has often been pointed out, is one of the great spiritual vehicles of Puritanism. And in writing his own spiritual pilgrimage in *Grace Abounding to the Chief of Sinners* Bunyan tells of his long travail, with many ups and downs, many crises, many despairs, and many moments when the divine cheerfulness breaks in. The ministry of Mr. Gifford, his baptism in the waters of the Ouse in 1653, were the prelude to a ministry of his own, first as a preacher and then as one exercising a genuine cure of souls.

Trouble came at the Restoration, for the local authorities were hostile to the Dissenting meetings, and on November 12, 1660, Bunyan was arrested at the beginning of a service. He could have got away: there had been some kind of warning, "there was whispering that that day I should be taken". But with courage he refused to go. "No, by no means. I will not stir: neither will I have the meeting dismissed for this. Come, be of good cheer. Let us not be daunted: our cause is good: we need not be ashamed of it. To preach God's word is so good a work, that we shall be well rewarded if we suffer for that." And perhaps not one of Bunyan's heroic characters—Standfast, Hopeful, Greatheart, Valiant for Truth—ever spoke fairer or more forthrightly than that.

He was imprisoned in the county gaol. And we think of

the burden which fell upon his wife, remembering Philip Guedalla's famous parody,

> Wives of great men all remind us
> We can make our lives sublime.

Bunyan knew what she had to bear. "I should often have brought into my mind the many hardships, miseries and wants that my poor Family was like to meet with, should I be taken from them, especially my poor blind child, who lay nearer to my heart than all I had besides." He was hardly treated and exempted from the Coronation amnesty in 1661. But gaol in the 17th century was a haphazard affair: it could be horrible, or it could be much more humane than any modern hygienic, inexorable prison. There were other Dissenters there: at one time a friendly gaoler let him go as far away as London, and he seems to have been allowed to go visiting with his fellow deacons. After 1668 he began to come out on parole, but he was re-arrested. Before his release in 1672 he had been elected by his fellow Baptists to be pastor of their Church. He was again imprisoned in 1677 for about six months. During his years of freedom he gained a great reputation as a powerful preacher. There is a famous description of him which matches the better of the surviving portraits:

> he was tall of stature, strong boned, though not corpulent, somewhat of a ruddy face, with sparkling eyes, wearing his hair on his upper lip, after the old British fashion: his hair reddish, but in his latter days time had sprinkled it with grey, his nose well set, but not declining or bending, and his mouth moderate large, his forehead something high and his habit always plain and modest.

Bunyan died in August 1688. As with Martin Luther, it was an errand of Christian reconciliation which led to fatal illness and to death. Bunyan was buried in Bunhill fields, in a plain if inelegant tomb, and there the pilgrim Crusader lies "like a warrior taking his rest".

Bunyan wrote very much: but most of his sixty-two works have little survival value. The Cautionary Tale of Mr. Badman, the too involved allegory of Mansoul, have their moments, but on the whole it is his *Grace Abounding* and *Pilgrim's Progress* which really count. It is not clear just when he wrote *Pilgrim's Progress*, and it seems that it must have been while he was imprisoned in the county gaol. It was entered at Stationer's Hall December 22, 1677, licensed February 18, 1678, and soon sold by Nathaniel Ponder in the Poultry, price 1s. 6d. Much time has been spent by many authors on possible pedigrees, on literary sources. Certainly the English Bible and Foxe's *Book of Martyrs* were the staple of his library. Yet, as Henri Talon has said in his superb study,

> It is not books that copy books, but souls that copy souls.

Bunyan was in one sense "just another" meckanick preacher: his book is "just another" homily about spiritual warfare, Christian pilgrimage. But what matters is wherein he differs from his kind. Here was a Christian writer, the greatest since Dante, with Dante's own capacity, the eyes that saw everything, that facility for concrete imagery which links both with Virgil and even more significantly with the parables of Jesus. For the greatness of *Pilgrim's Progress* is that it is not an allegory but a parable, or rather a series of parables. It lives just as it escapes being allegorical. If you turn to Bunyan's *Emblems*, the little allegories which he wrote for children, you will see that he can be as dull as anybody else. Take Number 36: "Upon the sight of a pound of candles falling to the ground", "the fallen candles do us intimate, the bulk of Gods elect in their lapsed state". But in *Pilgrim's Progress* at its best the teaching comes to us through and in some piece of human experience, or human character. There is much of the whole craft of Bunyan in that fine picture of an old Christian, Mr. Honest—"Not honesty in the abstract, but Honest is

G

my name". Macaulay was profoundly right in showing Bunyan's superiority to Spenser in this matter, and in saying that it is Bunyan's humanity which touches us all: and we might add, which has survived translation into a hundred languages. Only occasionally does the allegory run away with the story, and only now and then does the theology obtrude itself, as in that dreary walk by Hopeful and Christian when they leave Ignorance behind, and where they argue as two preachers will to the oblivion of the scenery. But when the allegory dwindles, then it is a parable: the story itself speaks, as in the famous fight with Apollyon and the journey through the Valley of Humiliation. Or there is the famous story of how Matthew is sick of the gripes, through eating green and forbidden fruit. Here is a story which any parent understands who has ever sat by a boy's bedside and tried to make him take his medicine. There is Dr. Skill, an interesting and recognizable blend of petulance and urbanity, and Christiana who knows what every mother knows and does what every mother has always done down to the same perennial, and always to be pardoned, fib. "And with that she touched one of the pills with the tip of her tongue. 'Oh, Matthew', said she, 'this potion is sweeter than honey. If thou lovest thy mother, if thou lovest thy brothers, if thou lovest Mercy, if thou lovest thy life, take it.'" And so Matthew swallows down his medicine, and unawares you and I have swallowed a good deal of sound Protestant theology. No wonder Coleridge called it a compendium of evangelical doctrine, and we shall be wise not to treat it as a long outmoded pious book for children. A Christian today may find a good deal of fruitful instruction in it for his soul's health. There are two ways of writing theology: one is that of St. Thomas Aquinas and Karl Barth, who spend a lifetime writing a huge "Summa" of Christian doctrine. But Bunyan's way is a way too, and rather handier for busy Christians.

So Bunyan's humanity is allied with his vision into human life. Henri Talon quotes the fine saying of Péguy about Victor Hugo, "He had the gift of being able to see creation as if it had just come from the hands of the creator." And next to his humanity we must surely put his tenderness. "Bowels becometh pilgrims." This is not to forget the sternness: the awful warnings, the catastrophes, the menaces, the foolish and evil characters, the dreadful last paragraph about Ignorance which seems almost to wreck the beauty of the magnificent climax of the dream. Yet chiaroscuro is an important element in painting, and Rembrandt and Bunyan and their 17th-century contemporaries know something about darkness in relation to light: what darkness can do to colour and to light, and what light does to darkness when it really shines. Strip the shadows from a Rembrandt, strip the toughness from the *Pilgrim's Progress*, and you have spoiled it all: a "larger hope" in our modern sentimental way would in the end drain all the strength. *Pilgrim's Progress* is built out of two immense images, that of pilgrimage and that of spiritual warfare, and the nerve of its power lies in the intermingling of the two: and that is not just Bunyan's peculiarity, it is the message of the Catholic Church.

That is not at all to justify Puritan theology, for like most 17th-century systems of thought it needs a good deal of "de-mythologizing". It is often said that "Second Parts" and sequels are never successful. But I own there are two great works, *Alice in Wonderland* and *Pilgrim's Progress*, where if I had to choose I would choose the second parts, though I am thankful that we have them both. Bunyan in the Second Part is an older, mellower Christian, who has learned and grown through his sorrows and his conflicts. Old Honest, Mercy, Mr. Despondency and his daughter Mistress Much Afraid, above all Mr. Fearing. It is deeply significant that of all 17th-century writers it is a Puritan who evokes most clearly and poignantly the gentleness of God, who carries the lambs in his bosom and gently leads those that are with young. There is no finer line about the Church in all Christian literature than that of the Shepherd on the Delectable Mountains:

"These mountains are Immanuel's land, and they are within sight of his city; and the sheep also are his, and he laid down his life for them."

Allied with these qualities, his humour. We know that Bunyan was on the defensive about it, that it displeased many, that there were long-faced Puritans who preferred new, bowdlerized versions, suitable, as one of them suggested, for handing round at funerals. Indeed, there is more than humour to be ponderously discussed, there is fun. Not only Shakespeare but W. W. Jacobs and P. G. Wodehouse might have been proud to have written the sketch with not a word too many or too few, of the courtship of Mercy by Mr. Brisk. The second edition of the *Pilgrim's Progress* adds some famous scenes, but these are not moralistic passages. Who save Bunyan would have gone to the trouble of altering the story of Giant Despair, to introduce Mistress Diffidence, and to give the whole story another slant by turning the giant into a henpecked husband who has to go over the day's events in bed at night, and get his marching orders for the coming day?

Pilgrim's Progress may never regain its hold upon Protestant devotion in the way in which it was read, say, in Victorian homes. But it may be hoped that it will not be left either to the literary students or the theologians. Those who read it know it and love it, will go on reading it for its own sake. A modern German writer, Hans Zehrer, has spoken of the typical character of our century of violence as "The Man in the Hut", the man who in our time has lost all his earthly possessions: goods, children, wife, possessions. The refugee, the displaced person, the man who sits in some gloomy, bleak transit camp faced with the two great questions, "Where do I come from? Where am I going?"

That is where Christian begins, and the famous opening of *Pilgrim's Progress* strikes sharply into the fear of modern man in the Atomic Age:

A man clothed with rags, with his face from his own house . . . and a great burden upon his back . . . and he brake out with a lamentable cry, saying "What shall I do?" . . .

"O my dear wife, and you the children of my bowels, I . . . am undone by reason of a burden that lieth hard upon me. Moreover I am for certain informed that this our city will be burned with fire from heaven."

Modern man, in the ruins of Hiroshima and Nagasaki, in the prisons of Europe, in the cities of Hungary, knows as poignantly as Christian the dilemma of human existence. But modern man, unlike Christian, has no book in his hand, he has no faith in Evangelist, and a heavenly city seems to him much more likely to be a mirage. The God-dimension is missing, and he does his thinking in a curious parody of Christian verities. He too moves along a road of human experience: meets mishap and disaster: knows what comforts comradeship and love, joy and laughter, may bring: knows the besetting impact of evil and temptation: moves inexorably towards the lonely experience of dying. But he cannot answer the questions "Whence?" or "Whither?"

Once again the Church has the vocation of map-making, of showing the estranged millions about her that they have a divine origin and a celestial destiny. Robert Lynd has said that about all great literature there is a note of homesickness. Here in *Pilgrim's Progress* there is the ultimate human nostalgia, for that City of God which is the restless heart's true home. And even the cynical, the unbelieving and half-believing who goes with Christian to the end of the road must be a little shaken, may tremble to see something like a gate and also some of the glory of the place, and glimpsing something of the company within the golden gates, may wish himself among them.

CHAPTER VI

ISAAC WATTS
AND HIS HYMNS

PURITANISM won its wars: and lost its peace. And yet perhaps the manner of its victory contained the seeds of its disasters. There was the victory of a religious cause by means of force of arms, culminating in the "cruel necessity" of the execution of King Charles I. For when we have said all that may and must be said on the Puritan side, there is the truth which Lord Eustace Percy suggests in his fine study of John Knox:

> How ruthless the religion of humanity can be. Of all the teachings of history, the clearest is this: that those who seek to realize ideal aims by force of law, are always unscrupulous and always cruel.

There was the victory not only by physical force but by moral force, that subtle temptation which was later also to befall Victorian Nonconformity, the attempt of the moralists to force the pace and to impose a pattern of moralistic legislation, either by law itself or by the pressure of an intense moral fervour, upon an unconvinced and unconverted majority, which begets an inevitable reaction. That, at the Restoration, the attitude of the King and of the Bishops, and their handling of the Puritans was as clever as it was morally disreputable, is true: on the other hand, the failure of Presbyterians and Independents to join hands in the moment of opportunity in 1660, resulted in disaster: then came the aftermath of the failure of the Savoy Conference, the immoralist reactions of public life and the application of the Clarendon Code, the exclusion from the

Church of the sons of the Puritans. These suffered hence-
forward a double stigma: they were suspect as rebels and
the sons of rebels (and repression and persecution begat
indeed a sturdy truculence among the rising generation of
Puritans, now excluded from the older Universities and
constrained to the seminary limitations of the Dissenting
Academies). And they were Dissenters, outside the national
religion, though sufficiently powerful to make inevitable
the toleration which came partially in 1689.

Isaac Watts belongs to the second generation of the
Nonconformists. And it is as a Dissenting divine that
we must think of him, rather than as the minor poet who
got into the Cambridge History of English Literature
because Dr Johnson thought more highly of him than
he ought to have done (but then he had borrowed several
hundreds of Watts's definitions for his great Dictionary and
so owed him a compliment or two). He was a divine of
learning and importance at a time when English Puritan
theology, and a strong part of Anglican too, was perilously
on the brink of the rationalist landslide towards Socinianism
and Unitarianism.

We may begin with the quiet dignity of the simple tomb
in Bunhill fields, which tells us how Isaac Watts himself
would fain have been remembered:

> Isaac Watts, D.D. Pastor of a Church of Christ in
> London, successor to the Rev. Mr. Joseph Caryl, Dr.
> John Owen, Mr. David Clarkson and Dr. Isaac Chaun-
> cey, after fifty years of feeble labours in the gospel,
> interrupted by four years of tiresome sickness, was
> at last dismissed to his rest. In uno Jesu ómnia. 2 Cor. 5.
> 8. "Absent from the body and present with the Lord."
> Col. 3. 4. "When Christ who is my life shall appear,
> then shall I appear with him in glory."

"Isaac Watts, D.D. Pastor of a Church of Christ in
London." There is a challenging, trumpet note about it.
Isaac Watts was born into the Confessing Church of the

17th century, his mother suckled him on the steps of the gaol in Southampton, inside which his father was in bonds for the gospel of Christ. He knew from babyhood the joy and tribulation of belonging to a Church "under the Cross". And when he became a minister it was of a Church whose pedigree went back to the Civil War, built by men who had come to know that if they feared God they need fear no earthly dignities, and that a dispensation had been given them to safeguard the crown rights in the Church of Jesus Christ. It is true that the heroic days were passing and that Isaac Watts was of the often fatal second generation of the epigoni, which spoke of the "old Puritans" much as we today speak of "the Nonconformist conscience" which under William III found toleration and prosperity and temptation. Yet we must not exaggerate. It is true that the period between 1688 and the failure of the '45 rebellion was one of triumph for the Protestant cause and that, as Bernard Manning has said, "Watts was one of those fortunate persons whose life coincides with the increasing triumph of his cause. The right people win. The wicked are cast down." Yet the dangers were there.

They loomed large enough at the end of the reign of Anne, when it seemed that a new era of persecution from Tory High Churchmen was to begin. There came the news of the Queen's illness and the almost unbearable suspense as to whether the Angel of Death would beat the Statute Book. There was the famous moment when the Rev. Thomas Bradbury's sermon was interrupted by a panting, excited visitor who leaned over from the gallery and dropped a handkerchief which was stared at by a fascinated congregation as it pyramided and parachuted its way down to the floor: but it was to the minister a pre-arranged signal which gave out the wonderful news, which by an ironic paradox has passed into history as the sum of all banalities, "Queen Anne is dead", and led him to push away his sermon and announce a psalm of thanksgiving that the Schism Act was defeated; though one can hardly believe the nice story that he immediately preached on the text "Go ye and bury this cursed woman: for she is a king's daughter".

But by and large the times were set fair when in 1702 young Isaac Watts was called to be minister of the most fashionable and notable Independent church in England. He had been a prodigy in childhood, saying "Books, books" as soon as he was old enough to cry for anything. At the age of 4 he learned Latin, Greek at 5, Hebrew at 10, and began verse at the age of 6 or 7, when he wrote verses for his mother, who was wont to reward her children with a farthing on such an occasion:

> I write not for a farthing, but to try
> how I your farthing writers could outvie

He then became the bright boy at the Free School, and the star in the Dissenting Academy of Mr. Thomas Rowe. Though the academies lacked a good deal of the depth and tradition of the classical learning of the universities, the exclusion of Dissent from Oxford and Cambridge had certain advantages, and notably in the cleaner break in the academies with the long rhetorical tradition of education, and the turning to the new scientific disciplines, philosophy, astronomy, mathematics, of the age of the Royal Society and of Isaac Newton. There were keen winds of scepticism beginning to blow, and Isaac Watts himself was sometimes almost scared by the logical conclusions of his own arguments.

> "Sometimes I seem to have carried reason with me, even to the camp of Socinus, but then John gives my soul a twitch and Paul bears me back again . . . almost to the tents of Calvin."

On the day that Isaac Watts accepted the call to his first church, King William III died. While he lived the Dissenters had been protected, and if they thought of him with the kind of grateful adulation with which the Fathers at

Nicea regarded the Emperor Constantine, and if we almost feel that Isaac Watts's poetic comparison of Dutch William with the Archangel Gabriel leaves the Archangel more than a little damaged, we must remember how near to triumph Rome had seemed in 1688, and how a Popish pretender was in the background for most of Watts's life. And then, suddenly, his health gave way. Instead of activity—though he did a considerable work throughout the years—illness became a dominant theme of his career. Though he was almost invalided out of the Christian warfare at the age of 24, he was to live to be the oldest Dissenting minister in London: but over most of that life he burned with a slow flame. He was ill in 1698, in 1701, then for four years 1712-6, again in 1729 and 1736; and the last years until 1748 were like many of their predecessors, full of anxiety, weakness and pain. I do not know the nature of the disorders, though fevers are mentioned and towards the end a paralytic stroke, and it seems that his illnesses touched his nerves, if not at the last his mind. So, instead of bustling into his first pastorate, Isaac Watts had to go wearily touring the spas, to Bath and thence to Tunbridge Wells— where one day staring out upon the Pantiles he beheld a vision of loveliness, in three young ladies of fashion, and wrote a poem on the fairest of them all, in whom we have all some slight interest, for she was Lady Spencer and she accounts for the Spencer in Winston Spencer Churchill.

But he kept his church, and an assistant was found for him, and he found hospitable friends among the wealthy laymen of the congregation. It was the turn of the century: the beginning of the great century of British trade and British expansion: when the middle class became indispensable and powerful, so that, much as the Government might dislike Dissenters, it could not do without their money. And so, one way and another, Dissenting laymen were readmitted to a share in public life. Sometimes they paid huge fines cheerfully: Sir John Hartopp paid £7,000 in the reign of James II. Sometimes they became Occasional Conformists and took the Sacrament at the parish church. No doubt some of them were far from admirable characters: like the famous Hopkins who left £300,000 and whose cold avarice got him the nickname "Vulture Hopkins,". But we have heard too much of the Nonconformist grocer who put sand in the sugar. We might turn from the fictional caricature to the two historical patrons of Isaac Watts: Sir John Hartopp, a business man with more than a taste for learning:-

> Mathematical speculations and practices were a favourite study with him in his younger years: and even to his old age he maintained his acquaintance with the motions of the heavenly bodies and light and shade whereby time is measured . . . but the Book of God was his chief study. He was desirous of seeing what the spirit of God said to men in the original languages. To this end he commenced some acquaintance with Hebrew when he was more than fifty years old.

He was not ashamed to own his Lord or his Lord's people, for he walked wearing his chains of office as Alderman to Mark Lane chapel. And Sir Thomas Abney, Lord Mayor of London and Member of Parliament, who on Lord Mayor's Show Day left the fashionable rout at Guildhall in the middle of the reception and went home to his house in Lime Street to conduct family prayers as usual, returning afterwards to the glittering assembly.

It was in the Abney home that Isaac Watts found refuge, in Stoke Newington. Daniel Defoe, who had studied in the village, comments in his *Tour of England and Wales* on the amount of building and rebuilding that was going on there and in other suburbs:

> All these . . . are in a few years so increased in buildings and so fully inhabited that there is no comparison to be made between their present and their past state . . . they are generally belonging to the middle sort of man-

kind, grown wealthy by trade and who still taste of London . . . many of these are immensely rich.

For a time Sir Thomas Abney had kept a country house at Theobalds and a town residence in the city, but his second wife brought him the new big house at Stoke Newington. You may still see its great gates, part of the local cemetery, while Abney House has disappeared and the spacious lawns have been replaced by an overcrowded cemetery and part of Clissold Park. The story is famous how Isaac Watts went to stay for the week-end and tarried thirty years, but Lady Abney's pretty compliment is worth re-telling, too:

> "Sir," she said, "what you term a long thirty years visit I consider the shortest visit my family ever had."

Here was Isaac Watts's home. For his brief romance with a Miss Singer was very soon dashed: and if it be not true that she did tell him, with reference to his small and rather unimpressive frame, that "she loved the jewel, but could not admire the casket", he seems to have been a day too late with his proposal, and instead of bestowing on him her hand, all he ever had from her was a vast mass of very inferior poetry through which he dutifully waded and loyally edited in later years.

This is how one of his friends described him:

> His stature was beneath the common standard, perhaps not above five feet or at most five feet two inches . . . his body was spare and lean, his face oval, his nose aquiline, his complexion fair and pale, his forehead, his cheek bones rather prominent, but his countenance on the whole by no means disagreeable. His eyes were small and grey . . . amazingly piercing and expressive . . . his voice rather too fine and slender but regular, audible and pleasant.

It was there, on October 4, 1738, that he was visited by

another little giant, John Wesley. All we know about this
is the tantalizing brevity of John Wesley's diary:

> 1.30 at Dr. Watts. Conversed. 2.30 Walked, singing,
> conversed.

We may guess part of the conversation, for Isaac Watts
had sent a contribution to help the distressed German
Protestants from Salzburg who had formed a settlement
just outside Savannah in Georgia, where John Wesley
had recently been missionary. And then there is the picture
of them walking under the trees, two plain, trim little men,
singing to one another their own and other people's hymns.

Outside his study he hung a Latin verse about the dangers
of uncharitable gossip: he knew the besetting sin of minis-
ters' studies and of the conversation of religious people.
The walls were well filled with brown leather-covered
volumes, but between them he hung his ever-growing
collection of engravings of famous men, some of them
autographed, while near the fireplace were two large sheets
of white paper, quite blank, with a Latin footnote for his
guests and which may roughly be translated, "This space
reserved for . . . ?" a hint to his visitors that they might,
if they chose, enlarge the collection.

I must stress his concern for pastoral care and for the
cure of souls. He once said that he would rather have
written Richard Baxter's *Alarm to the Unconverted* than
the whole of Milton's *Paradise Lost*. He was himself a fine
preacher in the great Puritan tradition, and many passages
in his sermons remind us of the fecundity of thought and
the wealth of imagery which made him the greatest of all
English hymn writers. He thought much about the art of
preaching and wrote on the subject for theological students
with a dry humour. Thus he contrasts two imaginary
student preachers: Polyramus and Fluvio. Polyramus goes
in for divisions and sub-divisions and "runs up the number
of them into 18thly or seven and twentiethly", and "when
I sit under his preaching I fancy myself brought into the

valley of Ezekiel's vision: it was full of bones and behold they were very many . . . and lo, they were very dry". Whereas Fluvio has no divisions at all and "glides over the ear like a rivulet of oil over polished marble . . . the attention is engaged in a gentle pleasure . . . but the hearer can give an enquiring friend scarcely any account of what it was that pleased him".

But it was no wonder that he turned more and more to writing, writing with the direct lucid style which came in with Dryden and Defoe. He wrote half a dozen textbooks, and one of them, the book on Logic, became the standard text at Oxford and Cambridge, Harvard and Yale. His book on astronomy and geography was a great success despite the doubtful advantage of a preface by an F.R.S., one of those expert prefaces which damn the author by suggesting him to be after all, the gifted amateur. Then there were the extraordinary *Philosophical Essays* which moved Mrs. Piozzi, Dr. Johnson's friend, to exclaim at one of the more turgid paragraphs:

> "This is like Ajax's Prayer in the Iliad: Scarce inferior to Homer in poetic expression. O Admirable Isaac Watts!"

Above all he was interested in the education of children: an ardent champion of the growing Charity School movement against the forces of oppression and obscurantism. His catechisms were famous throughout the world and were in their way revolutionary. He carried through a thorough grading of them by issuing one for children of 4, one for them at 5, one at 9, one at 11, with notes. He knew that children must be treated differently at different ages, and taught truths about God and their religion differently at different stages in their growth. And if it be true, as one distinguished Anglican authority once told me, that the right way to write a catechism is to imagine somebody aged 90 and write for him, there is after all a difference between treating old people as though they were children, and the great illusion of most educationists until modern times, that you must treat little children as though they were old men! And Isaac Watts knew the other half-truth, that children must be taught the same things, so that the Christian way is like a spiral staircase where we constantly return to the same themes, but at a new level and with a wider perspective.

And this brings us to his great achievement, his *Divine Songs for Children*, so that he became the all-time children's best seller before the advent of Miss Enid Blyton. Some of their lines have become almost proverbial: "Birds in their little nests agree", "Satan finds some mischief still for idle hands to do", though my generation comes to them across the *Cautionary Tales* and *Alice*, so that it is hard to take them seriously and to realize what an innovation and creative achievement it was when this great hymn writer could attempt "to sink the language to the level of a child's understanding and yet to keep it if possible above contempt".

So we have all smiled at

> Let dogs delight to bark and bite,
> For God hath made them so:
> Let bears and lions growl and fight,
> For 'tis their nature too.

But most of us have never even known that the hymn goes on to a verse as tender any mediaeval carol:

> Let love through all your actions run,
> And all your words be mild:
> Live like the blessed Virgin's Son,
> That sweet and lovely child:
> His soul was gentle as a lamb.

And, as with Wordsworth, the attempt at simplicity is sometimes overdone and achieves a bathos accentuated by changing word sense, as in the following caution against vanity of dress:

How proud we are! how fond to show
Our clothes and call them rich and new,
When the poor sheep and silkworms wore
That very clothing long before.

The tulip and the butterfly
Appear in gayer coats than I:
Let me be dressed fine as I will,
Flies, worms and flowers exceed me still.

At its best, as in the lullaby which is deservedly in the *Oxford Book of Carols*, there is a lovely simplicity:

Hush, my dear, lie still and slumber,
Holy angels guard thy bed,
Heavenly blessings without number
Gently falling on thy head.

A tender cradle hymn in which the mother contrasts the peaceful content of her sleeping child with the mean home of the Saviour in the stable:

See the lovely babe addressing:
Lovely infant, how he smiled:
When he wept the mother's blessing
Soothed and hushed the holy child.

So we turn to the hymns themselves. Watts was a genius and a revolutionary, and he saved the worship of Nonconformity, at a time when its theology was endangered by an insurgent rationalism. But he was no mere innovator. Like Tyndale and Cranmer and Luther, he took what was best in the past and carried it to a new level. Nonconformist worship had reached a dangerous stalemate. In the beginning of the Reformation, and especially in the Calvinist churches, the congregational singing of the Psalms was an immense gain to a worship otherwise saddened and sombred by the refusal of all musical and artistic aids to worship. Thus psalm singing became the main congregational singing for the Protestants and Puritans and the great mediaeval hymn tradition was not continued in England and Scotland as it was by Luther in Germany. Moreover, in the accepted versions of the Psalms by Sternhold and Hopkins and by Tate and Brady the attempt was made to set the Psalms to versions so literal as to be often rigid to the point of comedy.

Thus to anticipate our argument—compare the majestic verse of "Our God, our help in ages past".

Watts's rendering of Psalm 90:

> A thousand ages in thy sight
> Are like an evening gone,
> Short as the watch that ends the night
> Before the rising sun.

But in Sternhold and Hopkins it goes:

> The lasting of a thousand years,
> What is it in thy sight,
> As yesterday it doth appear
> Or as a watch by night.

Moreover—a feature of English Nonconformist worship which irked Watts very much and was to be prolonged in England by the semi-literacy of the first Methodists— the Psalms were droned out line by line, after the clerk had recited them, line by line, to the congregation. One wonders how long worship could have gone on at this poor dying rate. Against all this Isaac had revolted as a boy, and when his father taunted him, "What can you put in their place?" he wrote hymns, which were no mere re-shuffling of a rigid pattern of Scriptural phrases, but songs of praise to Christ, able to be sung joyfully by the great congregation. The Baptist William Keach had been a pioneer before him, but by and large it was Watts who was the innovating genius. And so his main achievement is twofold. First he turned the Jewish Psalms into Christian hymns. His preface to his new edition of the Psalms is a revolutionary manifesto:

H

David left a rich variety of holy songs, but rich as it is, it is still far short of the glorious things we Christians have to sing before the Lord.

To my judgment the royal author is most honoured when he is most intelligible, and when his admirable compositions are copied in such language as gives light and joy to saints that live two thousand years after him. . . .

And he goes on to point out how the Psalms sometimes impede Christian devotion because they are bound to a vocabulary reminiscent of things which at their best were but shadows of the better things to come in Christ:

Have not your spirits taken wing and mounted up to God and glory with the song of David on your tongue, but on a sudden the clerk has proposed the next line . . . with burnt offerings or hyssop with new moons and trumpets and timbrels in it, with confessions of sins you never committed, with complaints of sorrows you never felt, cursing such enemies as you never had, giving thanks for such victories as you never obtained and how have all your souls been discomposed at once and the strings of harmony all untuned. My design has been to accommodate the Book of Psalms to Christian worship, and to make them speak always the language of a Christian.

And if there is perhaps here a hint of the old Puritan prejudice against Anglican worship, and the Psalms which form so important a part of the structure of Mattins and Evensong, at least Isaac Watts offered a positive alternative.

Some of his versions are well known and well loved by all the English Churches. The fine version of Psalm 46 brought courage to at least one congregation in the London blitz who sang within forty-eight hours of seeing their little chapel in ruins,

> Let mountains from their seats be hurled
> Down to the deep and buried there,

Convulsions shake the solid world;
Our faith shall never yield to fear.

And another of them, "Our God, our help in ages past,"
is more than a hymn, it is an event in English history, and
part of our very national existence.

And second, though in time the first, for the hymns were
published in 1707 and the Psalms ten or twelve years later,
there were the hymns. Consider for a moment the Dissenting chapels of that day. They were not ugly, as the 19th
century was to bring ugliness in manifold forms into
Nonconformist worship: at their best they were neat and
dignified and simple and light. But sometimes they seemed
to be preaching boxes, and in the new manner of the late
17th and 18th centuries they left no dark corners to suggest
infinities, but squared the compass of the heavens in a
compact building which all could overlook. There were no
murals, no crucifix, no altars, no lights in the sanctuary. All
of the mystery and infinity of religion had to be suggested
by words. And here, almost in the nick of time, Isaac
Watts came to the rescue. A great Jesuit theologian,
Erich Przywara, in a treatise on the rationale of worship,
"Polarity", has suggested four indispensable notes of
Christian devotion: first the transcendence of God—or as
we might say, God afar off—and then the immanence of
God—God made near: and then the subjectivity of religion
—its inwardness and privateness: and then the objectivity,
the realness or thingness of it. Watts's hymns illuminate
and embody these great principles. Supremely among hymn
writers, not even excepting Charles Wesley, he suggests
the greatness of God, Calvin's God whose supreme quality
is "sovereign Grace", and the amazing condescension of
God visiting his people in his dear Son in a personal
intimacy which never becomes sentimental, since it is
almost always expressed in terms of the objectivities of
the divine promises and of the ordinances of Word and
Sacrament.

So the last verse of the great hymn,

> The Lord Jehovah reigns

with its fine conclusion:

> And can this mighty King of glory
> condescend?
> And will he write his name,
> "My Father and my friend"?
> I love his name, I love his word,
> Join all my powers
> And praise the Lord.

And this sense of the greatness of God brings with it a sense of the vastness and majesty of the universe.

"Watts sees the Cross", says Bernard Manning, "as Milton had seen it, planted on a globe hung in space, surrounded by the vast distances of the Universe. He sees the drama in Palestine prepared before the beginning of time and still decisive when time has ceased to be. There is a sense of the spaciousness of nature, of the vastness of time, of the dreadfulness of eternity."

> A glance of thine runs through the globe,
> Rules the bright words and moves their
> frame.
> Of light thou formst thy dazzling robe,
> Thy ministers are living flame.
>
> How shall polluted mortals dare
> To sing thy glory or thy grace?
> Beneath thy feet we lie afar
> And see but shadows of thy face.

And sometimes in hymns which have had as a whole no survival value we have the same thought suggested in some magnificent opening line like

> Bright King of Glory, dreadful God.

Or an entire verse:

> He that can dash whole worlds to death
> And make them when he please,
> He speaks and that almighty breath
> Fulfils his great decrees.

And we couple with space, his thought of time, and of the transitoriness of human life which, as Lord Morley pointed out in a great passage in his *Recollections*, was one of the supreme intuitions of the Hebrew mind.

Perhaps Isaac learned this the hard way: on a sick bed. For among the poems written in his illness there is one which is more than a little moving, in its indication of an experience of weariness and pain.

> My watch, the solitary kind companion of
>   my imprisonment,
> My faithful watch, and with a short
>   repeated sound
> Beats like the pulse of time and numbers
>   off my woes a long succession, while the
>   finger
> Slow, moving, points out the slow moving
>   minutes,
> The slower hands the hours. O thou dear
>   engine,
> Thou little brass accountant of my life,
> Would but the mighty wheels of heaven and
>   nature
> Once imitate thy movements, how my hand
>   should
> Drive thy dentured pinions round their
>   centres
> With more than tenfold flight and whirl
>   away
> These clouded wintry suns, these tedious
>   moons,
> These midnights.   *December,* 1712

The thought finds an almost comic banality in one hymn:

> The present moments just appear,
> Then slide away in haste,
> That we can never say "they're here",
> But only say "they're past".

But here it is again, a blend of objectivity given in Scripture, and of personal experience as perfect as a Bach chorale:

> Time, like an ever rolling stream,
> Bears all its sons away,
> They fly forgotten as a dream
> Dies at the opening day.

But with this there is a sense of personal intimacy with God, a strain of inward religion which links him with George Herbert and with the great mystics. It was the stupendous claim of Dissenting worship to embody this principle of intimacy (so that at its best not awe but wonder is the keynote of Nonconformist worship), the solemn claim that a man may speak with God as a man speaketh to his friend. In his *Guide to Prayer*, which has been reprinted in recent years, Watts stresses the dignity and privilege of prayer, but he also goes on to tell the Christian:

> Seek earnestly a state of friendship with him with whom you converse, and labour after a good hope and assurance of that friendship. How unspeakable is the pleasure in holding converse with so infinite, so almighty and so compassionate a friend.

So in one of the loveliest of all devotional hymns, "My God, the Spring of all my joys".

> The opening heavens around me shine
> With beams of sacred bliss,
> If Jesus shows his mercy mine
> And whispers I am his.

And there is a story of how a great Victorian Christian

in his last hours, and amid great bodily pain, leaped in mind
to the verses which follow:

> My soul would leave this heavy clay
> At that transporting word,
> Run up with joy the shining way
> To see and praise my Lord.
>
> Fearless of hell and ghastly death,
> I'd break through every foe.
> The wings of love and arms of faith
> Would bear me safely through.

It is not for nothing that the first Methodist hymn book
began with a section entitled "The Pleasantness and Ex-
cellence of Religion", for the Wesleys with Isaac Watts had
a religion of happiness and cheerfulness.

> Questions and doubts be heard no more,
> Let Christ and joy be all our theme.

Or the familiar

> Come, ye that love the Lord,
> And let your joys be known.
>
> .   .   .   .   .   .
>
> Then let our songs abound
> And every tear be dry,
> We are marching through
>   Emmanuel's land
> To fairer worlds on high.

And the startling line

> Religion never was designed
> To make our pleasures less.

The objectivity of this inward religion is safeguarded
by its constant reference to the great affirmations of Christian creed: to the doctrine of the Trinity, to the Person

and Work of Christ and his intercession for us, as in the lovely verses:

> Christ the heavenly lamb
> Takes all our sins away,
> A sacrifice of nobler name
> And richer blood than they.
>
> My faith would lay her hand
> On that dear head of thine
> While like a penitent I stand
> And here confess my sin.

Or on the great theme of the Plan of Salvation itself, with its sombre beginning:

> Plunged in a gulf of dark despair
> We wretched sinners lay,
> Without one cheerful beam of hope
> Or spark of glimmering day.

And its triumphant exordium:

> O for this love, let rocks and hills
> Their lasting silence break,
> And all harmonious human tongues
> The Saviour's praises speak.

Nor is this a mere individual piety. The theme of the "Communion of Saints" is a frequent undertone, and evoked for Watts one of the finest hymns for all the saints,

> Give me the wings of faith to rise
> Within the veil and see
> The saints above, how great their joys
> How bright their glories be.

And he wrote a whole series of hymns for the sacramental ordinances, while it is not to be forgotten that perhaps the greatest of all Christian hymns, "When I survey the wondrous Cross", was written for the sacrament of the holy communion and presupposes the Nonconformist devotion to and interpretation of the eucharist.

Of course he wrote some bad verse and some bad hymns. But when we remember that he wrote about 700 hymns and Charles Wesley some 7,000, the proportion of limping, maimed lines in both are surprisingly small. There are hymns about which the fashions have changed, and hymns whose words have become quaint and silly to us. And both of these together perhaps, in his patriotically religious hymns.

Here again Bernard Manning has wise words for us:

> In making David speak like a Christian, Watts most properly made him speak also like an Englishman, not to say like an 18th-century Whig. Watts equates, that is to say, Palestine, Israel, Judaea, Jerusalem with Great Britain.

Isaac Watts's grandfather had been a captain under Admiral Blake and had been killed when his ship was blown up. He had inherited the sturdy patriotism of Milton, with its concomitant Protestant distrust of Rome. So he writes a hymn for Guy Fawkes day:

> Their secret fires in caverns lay,
> And we the sacrifice,
> But gloomy caverns strove in vain
>
> To scape all searching eyes.
> Their dark designs were all revealed,
> Their treason all betrayed.

And there is the quaint picture of William III looking down from his indubitable bliss to hail the accession of the second George:

> Come, light divine and grace unknown;
> Come aid the labours of the throne.
> Let Britain's golden ages run
> In circles lasting as the sun.

> Bid some bright legions of the sky
> Assist the glad solemnity;
> Ye hosts that wait on fav'rite kings,
> Wave your broad swords and clap your wings.
>
> Then rise and to your realms convey
> The glorious tidings of the day:
> Great William shall rejoice to know
> That George the Second rules below.

Then there are the hymns about worms, though there is something to be said for this vermicellian theology, since the worm represents the thingness of creation, and the vast antithesis between the infinite Creator and the things that he has made.

If Watts had learned with Milton how to employ proper names and geographical localities in a great roll call, he sometimes anticipates the painful bathos of Wordsworth in introducing prosaic names, as the famous Wordworthian

> Spade, with which Wilkinson has tilled his land.

And so Watts celebrated the deaths of two great Dissenting laymen:

> Great Gouge to dust, how doleful is the sound.
> Sion grows weak and England poor.

and the even less fitting

> Abney expires: a general groan.

Then there are the lines which sound quaint to us but may not have done to the first readers:

> Come, saints, and drop a tear or two
> On the dear bosom of your God.

And the equally casual sounding reference to the Ascension,

> Well, the Redeemer's gone!

And this:

God is my portion and my joy,
His counsels are my light;
He gives me sweet advice by day
And gentle hints by night

I cannot here argue the relative merits of Isaac Watts and
Charles Wesley, even though Watts himself said he would
rather have written Wesley's great poem "Wrestling
Jacob",

Come, O thou traveller unknown,

than all his own hymns. But as a Methodist I may honestly
concede that on the whole I think Watts the greater hymn
writer, though both together are incomparable, and should
still form the staple of Nonconformist hymn singing, as
they stand head and shoulders above the whole spate of
sentimental and precious ditties of the 19th and 20th
centuries.

Isaac Watts was that meanest of all 18th-century figures,
the figure of fun in its literature, the domestic chaplain of
a wealthy patron, not quite a servant but equally certainly
not quite a gentleman. And yet these are the robes that
wrap a saint. Isaac Watts was a scholar and a gentleman
and a great divine. Above all he was a Christian who
learned the hard way to fight the fight of faith. Lying on his
bed watching the minutes tick away: or in the small hours
longing for the dawn, throbbing with his own aching body,
he knew in the literal sense of the grave New Testament
word the "agony" of the Christian warfare, the struggle
with doubt and with complaining, that same endurance
which worketh patience, that same patience which worketh
hope, and that same hope which putteth not to shame;
until having done all, he could catch that final word which
he had inscribed on his tomb, "dismissed—at last". Just
think of the setting. Abney House, Stoke Newington,
amid the tradesmen and the wealthy bankers and the
incessant hammering of workmen, where year in year out
during his life men and women acted the Parable of the

Rich Fool, where they pulled down their barns to build greater, and where they retired to take their ease only to find their souls required of them in the moment of death. And here, among the prosperous and the discreetly fashionable and the worldly minded, there walked a man who knew supremely this one fact, that if the earthly house of our tabernacle be dissolved, we have a building from God, a house not built with hands, eternal in the heavens: who had had to learn to look beyond this life, beyond the seen horizons of time and space. When he lay in bed one long dreary winter, his friends tried to cheer him with the thought of spring:

> "Look out", they cry,
> "Beyond these glooming damps, while winter
>   hangs
> Heavy on nature and congeals her powers.
> Look cheerful forward to the vital influence
>   of returning spring."

Yet he would not be comforted, but, like the Pilgrim Fathers, he "lifted his eyes to the heavens his dearest country", "and quieted his spirit".

> *There* is a land of pure delight,
> Where saints immortal reign;
> Infinite day excludes the night,
> And pleasures banish pain.
>
> There everlasting spring abides,
> And never-withering flowers;
> Death, like a narrow sea, divides
> That heavenly land from ours.

WILLIAM TYNDALE, Thomas Cranmer, John Foxe, John Milton, John Bunyan, Isaac Watts: an archbishop and a tinker, a scholar, a poet, a historian, a divine. Each made something which mankind has not willingly let die. There came a moment when each of them handled the brave new pages, in their shining whiteness, running their fingers down the binding which cradled this newborn offspring of their mind—with no assurance beyond that of faith that their work would prolong their speech for many generations, hold converse with millions yet unborn. Between them, these works of their mind and heart laid quickening impress on English religion, and have enriched the life of many churches. Above all they witness that, despite the sins of Christian men and the failings of the Church, despite the shouting and the clamour of schism and separation, the clouds and thick darkness of the days of judgment, the Lord of the Church has always stood in the midst devising good gifts beyond our hope, deserving and understanding.

ABOUT BOOKS

THE main thing, as I have said, is to read these books themselves. About most of them there are good, not too technical, studies. On the English Bibles, the two invaluable books by J. F. Mozley, *William Tyndale* (1938) and *Coverdale and his Bible* (1953), and the more technical studies of Professor Butterworth of Philadelphia, are of great interest. On Cranmer, A. F. Pollard is still to be read. Outstanding among the studies provoked by the fourth centenary of his martyrdom are the volume by W. G. Bromiley and the lectures given at Lambeth by Professors N. Sykes and E. C. Ratcliffe (1956). J. F. Mozley's *John Foxe and his Book* (1940) is a most timely and able study which I have shamelessly pillaged. The best edition of Foxe is the eight-volume Victorian edition, which is a mine of first-hand documents, more enthralling than all the secondary studies. About Puritanism in general, *The Rise of Puritanism* by William Haller is now indispensable, and the introduction to Perry Miller's anthology *Puritanism*. Out of a multitude of studies on Milton there are three readable modern essays: F. E. Hutchinson's luminous *Milton and the English Mind* (Teach Yourself History series, 1946), C. S. Lewis's *Preface to Paradise Lost*, and E. W. Tillyard's *Milton*. On Bunyan, the English translation of Henri Talon's splendid *John Bunyan* (1951) and the recent study by Roger Sharrock, *John Bunyan* (Hutchinson's University Library). Macaulay is to be read on Milton and on Bunyan. And Vaughan Williams's music to *Pilgrim's Progress* will tell you more things than most books. Watch out for second-hand copies of Watts's hymns, in addition to reading Bernard Manning's *Hymns of Wesley and of Watts* (1942).

Date Due

FEB 2 1966

NOV 1 1966

FEB 1 0 1977

JUN 18 1981

DEC 8 1995

APR 3 0 2008

PRINTED IN U.S.A.